Now That
My Father
Lies Down
Beside Me

[handwritten inscription]

To Harry

and our Italian

Hans

Love. *[signature]*

SC 17. 01

Now That My Father Lies Down Beside Me

New & Selected Poems
1970 – 2000

Stanley Plumly

ecco

An Imprint of HarperCollinsPublishers

A hardcover edition of this book was published in June 2000 by The Ecco Press.

New poems first appeared in the following publications: *Atlantic Monthly*—"Naps," "Piano," "Strays"; *Gettysburg Review*—"November 11, 1942–November 12, 1997"; *Kenyon Review*—"Comment on Thom Gunn's 'In Santa Maria Del Popolo' Concerning Caravaggio's *The Conversion of St. Paul*," "In the Old Jewish Cemetery in Prague"; *The New Bread Loaf Anthology of Contemporary American Poetry*—"Catbird Beginning with a Cardinal"; *Ploughshares*—"Sickle"; *Poetry*—"Kunitz Tending Roses," "Wight"; *Slate*—"Cheer," "Grievers," "Turn, Counterturn, Stand"; *Southern Review*—"Cardinal," "Movie."

The epigraph is from Wallace Stevens's "The Owl in the Sarcophagus."

First Ecco paperback edition published in December 2001

Designed by Nancy Singer Olaguera

The Library of Congress has catalogued the hardcover edition as follows:

Plumly, Stanley.
    Now that my father lies down beside me : new & selected poems,
1970–2000 / Stanley Plumly.—1st ed.
        p. cm.
    ISBN 0-06-019659-9
    I. Title.
PS3566.L78 N69 2000
811'.54—dc21   99-057297

ISBN 0-06-093805-6 (pbk.)

01 02 03 04 05 ❖/RRD 10 9 8 7 6 5 4 3 2 1

It is a child that sings itself to sleep,
The mind, among the creatures that it makes,
The people, those by which it lives and dies.

—Stevens

Contents

Author's Note

These poems are in reverse chronological order of publication, beginning with new poems and including selections from *The Marriage in the Trees* (1997), *Boy on the Step* (1989), *Summer Celestial* (1983), *Out-of-the-Body Travel* (1977), *Giraffe* (1973), and *In the Outer Dark* (1970).

Grievers

Like some dreams, they appear, then reappear,
cloistered in the space of their own wounding,
their public mourning, their gravity's gray coat.
Even at a distance, as if drawn by being seen,
they come straight at you, the almost-elegant woman
in the aisle, the tall young birdlike silent
weeping man. And no one need have died, no one
you know, to know their voices and half-faces,
the scent of the spirit passing, for whom blood
on the door or blessing means nothing. But, then,
everyone died or didn't, who calls to you in sleep
after your back is turned. In the parable,
like the dream, you're all the characters,
though come the day, in real life, you must choose.

...m or fantasy I see my mother,
having put me down, leaning over me,
pulling the door shut twice, and if I rise
again, locking it. In school we were told
to put our heads down on the desks and think
of it as prayer or to lie on our left
sides on the floor, an inch between the pound
weight of the heart and passage of the earth.
We were told to listen to the silence,
not to talk, and breathe in slowly, slowly,
and pretend, if we had to, it was dark.
Already on our own we'd learned to study
out the window, to cogitate the tree
within the cloud, the long sunlit fingers
of the crow, and how to hold an object
in the mind and let it turn until it
turned the other life it wanted, the way
a doorknob with its facet-gaze of glass
becomes a diamond or a crystal,
and as you fall asleep, disintegrates,
snow in a paperweight. And now we were
intuiting sleeping in the future,
the disconnected nights, the dawn-light wakings,
the shadow puzzles clouding up the windows,
the hardwood study table and a chair,
gravity's floor—a lifetime's worth of all
the afternoons we'd lose or lose part of
trying to recover what was lost. So
we'd use our hands and arms to blind the eyes,
and then the mind to separate ourselves.
Then wait the voice outside calling our return,

the same voice as the moment of instruction:
to lie down in the middle of the day,
dream fragmentary, dusk-enhancing dreams,
be the body-of-the-one-looked-upon,
come back to life, O startled, distant child.

Piano

It must have been Lisa's voice
since she was waiting when we got there,
the bay doors barely open and her white
face running the bars along her stall.
Then Lisa brought her out into the hall
to brush her down in order to show
the wood sheen under the dust and how
the tension of the body, if she stood
still long enough, could make her look
like she was floating standing. And given
time, in the broken bird light falling
from the loft, she seemed to float,
nodding and letting her neck, a third
of all of her, bend to the floor,
where she swept, with little breaths,
each loose and useless piece until
she found the somewhere solid that
she wanted, striking the heavy air
to let us know, marking the place
to tell us, in a second, she could fly.
Her body had already started to shine,
but it was her blaze that gave her eyes
their depth against the touch and Lisa's
soft talk, that gave the eyes their depth.
And it was the eyes that sometimes flared
against the words. Lisa said she was wild
because she was young. And bored too
when she couldn't get out, yet never bored
the way some horses dance from side to side,
spelling their weight, pressing their radiant,
stalled foreheads into the walls, or the way

some horses disappear inside, having
drawn and redrawn circles. The barn was
full of the noise and silences of horses.
And filled with Lisa's voice in counter-
point: and Lisa's horse's stillnesses—
like love or what love's moment's stillness
really is, hands-high, and restless.

November 11, 1942–
November 12, 1997

My friend's body walking toward me
down the Pullman passage of his hallway.
He's naked as if he's just risen
from a bath and forgotten what it is
he's supposed to do next. He looks cold,
candle-white, with a sort of sunburn
on his face, especially his mouth,
which is open on a vowel. And there
seems to be an almost visible vertical
line drawn through him, so that half
of him is taller, half in tow.
It must be afternoon, since the daylight
is going and the doorway behind him
disappearing. Now it's colder.
Now I realize that for the longest time
I've been waiting for him, and need
to think of something, and that
he's expecting it, the way silence
sometimes promises. Then suddenly
he's in front of me, and I can see
how damp he is, how anointed with oil,
how all the color's focused in the eyes,
how the coral of the brain shines through
the forehead. And though he doesn't say so,
because he never would, I'm sure he wants me
to hold him, say his name, make him warm.
But when I try he puts his hand inside
his heart and offers me the stone,
then the Armistice poppy, and then
the bowl of bright arterial blood.

And from where the scar is, where they
saved his life and failed, the umbilical
intestine, impurities and purities of kidneys
and the liver, the two lungs out of breath,
and breath itself, cupped till it runneth over.

Turn, Counterturn, Stand

He's dressed like a patient,
naked to the waist, in bottoms like pajamas.
And hooked by invisible wire to a monitor hooked
to an amplifier. All of this onstage, like intensive
care, the badge of his connection at the center
of his chest, recording and rendering his pulse.
His heart is the dancer, and its muscle the music
that rises and subsides: each searching step, each
turn, each somersault and curl, each sudden rest.
Baryshnikov is fifty, but older, paler in the lights.
You hear his heart literally leap in the machine-
magnified midair. He won't come down, then all
at once he will.

When I bend to hear my parents'
hearts or lean against a wall to hear my friend's,
it's like water in a shell held tightly to the ear:
salt blood and ocean emptiness and wind, vena cava,
almost still. The last thing you want to hear is
the sound of your own worn heart. It has a signature,
a silence, like a voice or fingerprint, the heart
line of the graph the abstract of a mountain range
or large waves coming in, repeated and repeated and
repeated—a child's idea of drawing, a child's
obsessive dance or nursery rhyme, yet years and years
of listening to this child, who will not change
but does.

When I remember what it was like
to see them in the wards, impaled in bed and wired,
every orifice acknowledged, every innocence corrupted

and exposed, when I think of the awful trembling
passed by hand, the dry white chemical breath of what
was said, the skeletal skin so ghostly it seemed
they'd already gone—that God, in His Infinite Mercy,
had pulled their sick hearts out, bled them, drained
them, kissed the dead weight from the bones, that
I was looking into graves that were my parents—
when I think of them I think of my friend with no one
there those hours he had to suddenly lie down and
listen to his pulse.

Kunitz Tending Roses

Naturally he doesn't hear too well,
so that when he's kneeling he's really
listening at the very mouth of the flower.
And the feeling in his hands, his sense
of touch, seems gloved if not quite gone,
though when he bleeds he takes a certain
notice, wipes it away, then moves on.

And winter eyes. The old have passion's
winter eyes, which see with a pointillist
chill clarity, but must look close, as his do,
petal by petal, since the work is tactile
visual: Cadenza, Blaze, Red Fountain climbing
or like free-standing rhododendron,
sunset gold Medallion, scarlet Maiden.

His body bends depending on the height
and cluster or, on a perfect scale, the stature
of the rose, which, like the day, declines
continually: meaning that toward evening
he almost disappears among the fragrance,
gala, and double flesh of roses: or when
he's upright, back to the sun, is thin

enough to see through, thorn and bone.
Still, there he is, on any given day,
talking to ramblers, floribundas, Victorian
perpetuals, as if for beauty and to make us
glad or otherwise for envy and to make us
wish for more—if only to mystify and move us.
The damasked, dusky hundred-petaled heart.

Interrogate the rose, ask the old,
who have the seminal patience of flowers,
which question nothing, less for why we ask:
Enchanter, Ember, Blood Talisman, something
to summarize the color of desire, aureate
or red passion, something on fire to hold
in the hand, the hand torn with caring.

In the Old Jewish Cemetery in Prague

Winter riot of waves the way these stones
pile up, as if the dead, twelve deep in places,
had risen cold and left in anger. Something
threatening in their supernatural overlap
and angle, too alive, awkward, accidental,
some pushed hard from under, like the roots,
some dropped harder, broken with the rain,
under the limes and brooding maples—limestone,
sandstone, rose Silvenec marble ruined.

At *The Watering of the Horses of the Sun*
Apollo holds the water in a shell from
which one blazing stallion drinks, while
holding off three others breathing fire
with a hand and the pure power of his body—
this in bas-relief above the double stable
doors of the eighteenth-century Hotel de Rohan.
And clouds. Le Lorrain has built his story
at the source, both rain and horses coming

out of clouds, with the sun-god almost casual
between, in pockmarked pearl, sepulchral stone
but full of the life of the sky. When you
stand in the middle of the ghetto graves
and look straight up you can see why the dead
hate weather, why blue is the color of the
spirit rising, light the weightless moment
we see through. Stone is the shade of memory,
snowfall, dust, the piling and the drift.

Comment on Thom Gunn's *"In Santa Maria Del Popolo"* Concerning Caravaggio's The Conversion of St. Paul

As much as art about seeing in the dark
and when the setting sun will bring the painting
back to life from where it hangs in the chapel's
night recess, invisible except its spectral
parts, which look detached because the painter's
blacked the world out before he's set the candle
on the ladder, his single source of light
to shape an animal and two men out of shadows.

You say you're waiting for the sun to pull
the parts together—beyond their sexual, other-
worldly glow—to make the subject whole that shows
a man, fallen from a height, humbled and converted,
blessed or cursed too brilliantly by vision.
Yet *hardly enlightened* is your conclusion
once the enlightening sun arrives and you
can leave, passing obscure among believers.

My comment is I guess I couldn't wait,
either for sunset or the risk of dark, so put
my lire in the lumen box to see more or less
what you saw: a tall, pale pinto still confused
by the event, head bowed, right foreleg raised
in step; the dumb, distracted groom holding
the horse in place; night or nothingness;
and Saul, lying on his back, still falling,

struck blind by brilliant light inside his
head, the wings of his arms lifted to embrace

what is or isn't there—fear, then worse than fear,
blind faith—or lifted the way we fall to certain
death, believing we will rise from what we dream,
changed, twice alive, or at least unafraid,
as you believe the dreaming of last sunlight
through a window or coins dropped for a candle.

Strays

They'd show up at evening, with the change
of light, between a long day and supper,
close to the road or edge of the yard,
heads low, half starved, but quick as crows.
If you fed them, left meat scraps out at night,
they'd come back hungrier, and if you didn't,
if you ignored them or threw stones, they'd
simply back away, wary, starving, waiting
for dark in order to raid the smoking ashes
of the garbage, sometimes alone or in pairs,
sometimes in cerberus three-headed numbers.
They seemed almost to live somewhere, and near,
as certain of their ground as neighbors.

Serious neighbors shot them or tried poison,
while my father went to gather what he could
into the cowbed of his truck to be ferried.
Dogs that year were let out everywhere,
mongrels, pets, freak accidents, some with
mange or worse, the year of the holiday
death counts, the year somebody driving fast
blind-sided one in front of the house,
sent it flying all at once over the car:
it rose where it fell, where nobody wanted
to touch it since it acted still alive,
its puffed pink tongue lolling in its blood,
its canine neutral eye rolled over white.

We'd seen death before, and death brought back
to life, the spirit arm or leg of what was
missing from a boy, the mouth of the polio

friend breathing again, the ice of her face
on fire. But this was filled, unbroken flesh
continuous, the matted hair and open sores
unchanged. Somebody said, and I wished I'd
said it, let's find a place and bury it,
which nobody wanted to do, for fear of rabies
or a dog's disease. Finally one of the fathers
took a hind in each warm hand and dragged
the animal dead weight over to the shoulder
where serious crows and flies resurrect.

Wight

In the dark we disappear, pure being.
Our mirror images, impure being.

Being and becoming (Heidegger), being and
nothingness (Sartre)—which is purer being?

Being alone is no way to be: thus
loneliness is the test of pure being.

Nights in love I fell too far or not quite
far enough—one pure, one impure being.

Clouds, snow, mist, the dragon's breath on water,
smoke from fire—a metaphor's pure being.

Stillness and more stillness and the light locked
deep inside—both pure and impure being.

Is is the verb of being, I the noun—
or pronoun for the purists of being.

I was, I am, I looked within and saw
nothing very clearly: purest being.

Movie

Days I drove those distances it was night most of the time, the great highway dark the dark around the dials, new snow starlike on the thick black ice, ice starlit on the mountains, and the towns, the star-towns in the valleys spread for miles below the highest abstract elevations where I'd stop to scrape the windshield and let the wind wake me up, tempted just to stand there, at one with the clarity and snow, willing to join the star-configured cold come colder from Orion and the flooded Heavenly Waters' glittering and nothing like the glare through the negative of snow and sand salt mixed to mud and almost wiped away, each sweep of the wipers different, indifferent, on and off again, with the night-staggered oaks sending the last of their dead leaves down to confuse whatever else was lost in the headlights, the dust of ice forming at the edges and the window corners, the senses shutting slowly, one by one, the dark running its finger cold across the forehead, then the drifting in and out of falling, or not falling, not drifting off to sleep to voices on the radio, sleepers in their sleeplessness with hosts, or someone in the mirror off the road lighting up a flare already fading or the eyes, in their loneliness, focused on the wall, solid, liquid, black but permeable, since if you drove all night you'd never get there and if you didn't you'd never get there or if you crossed the median or hit the rail or caught the ice, impacted and enameled, if you slipped in thought and listened to yourself, if you talked to the desolate traffic coming on, if you wept, if you closed your eyes, if you went at the speeds of light and vanishing or simply pulled over to wait it out, the sun on the right rising somewhere, cupped in a wave, lifted and spilled, if you simply pulled over now where it's bright, got out of the car and started to walk, each difficult step disappearing in snow, if all that you did was get out of the car you'd never get there.

Cheer

Like the waxwings in the juniper,
a dozen at a time, divided, paired,
passing the berries back and forth, and by
nightfall, wobbling, piping, wounded with joy.

Or a party of redwings grazing what
falls—blossom and seed, nutmeat and fruit—
made light in the head and cut by the light,
swept from the ground, carried downwind, taken. . . .

It's called wing-rowing, the wing-burdened arms
unbending, yielding, striking a balance,
walking the white invisible line drawn
just ahead in the air, first sign the slur,

the liquid notes too liquid, the heart in
the mouth melodious, too close, which starts
the chanting, the crooning, the long lyric
silences, the song of our undoing.

It's called side-step, head-forward, raised-crown, flap-
and-glide-flight aggression, though courtship is
the object, affection the compulsion,
love the overspill—the body nodding,

still standing, ready to fly straight out of
itself—or its bill-tilt, wing-flash, topple-
over; wing-droop, bowing, tail-flick and drift;
back-ruffle, wingspread, quiver and soar.

Someone is troubled, someone is trying,
in earnest, to explain; to speak without
swallowing the tongue; to find the perfect
word among so few or the too many—

to sing like the thrush from the deepest part
of the understory, territorial,
carnal, thorn-at-the-throat, or flutelike
in order to make one sobering sound.

Sound of the breath blown over the bottle,
sound of the reveler home at dawn, light of
the sun a warbler yellow, the sun in
song-flight, lopsided-pose. Be of good cheer,

my father says, lifting his glass to greet
a morning in which he's awake to be
with the birds: or up all night in the sleep
of the world, alive again, singing.

Catbird Beginning with a Cardinal

First the all-red male arrives, in order to attract attention,
and once it's safe, the softer, buff-brown female.
They sit as a pair for less than the time it takes to see them.
Survival skills. None in the hand worth two in the tree.
And the mockers, even faster, split second by split second,
conspicuous as semaphore and flight-song.
Still, if you sing well enough, disappear enough,
and speak in a granular dove sort of gargle—and come alone—
the slate-gray, black-capped catbird, mewling along the arbor,
seems friendly, even catchable, if only captive,
or at least capable of being company,
since it isn't shy when it should be
and is susceptible to charm.
And trying to charm or catch one
wouldn't be an entirely alien if wild idea—
not so much to touch as to be proximate, in the presence of,
but close to the extent that if it let you
you might stroke its black felt cap or run a finger down a wing
or feed it suet or a berry from the holly
or talk to it as if it were the copy of the namesake of the cat
who sits outside the window in the rain like a ghost wanting in,
or, last resort, address it as a soul in transmigration,
one outsider to another, lost between locations—
though, on second thought, an old and flawed idea,
less because impossible than sentimental
in the worst domestic-garden-variety way,
failing to account for fundamental differences,
the obvious and not-so-clear genetics and odd genius,
the arrow of the tongue,
the nature of its eye and what it hears,

the sometime fever in the brain,
the hollowing of bone,
the graphite pencil-blue transparency of wings
opened like a greeting, then erased,
then quickly drawn again.

Cardinal

Against the green the line in red
the eye makes in order to keep up,
the thing least visible the moment
you see it. The afterimaging
the way you hear it too, two or three
in sequence or at once, as if when
you heard them they were there.

And against the back-lit, tonal
scale of the sky, at the laurel
height of the leaves, the broken
outlines of oak and yellow poplar,
drawn, in their moment, on the air.
No, since it's late and chill,
written in ink dissolve. Then

the night-sounds starting, and
the little bit of wind there was,
set and sealed. Then a fire-flint
closing call. And hour by falling
hour, patience and listening,
and in a while, toward morning
the fine still rain of the dew.

2

Bird that was brilliant flying,
evensong just whistling, dry gold
leaf that held, images and signs
against the dark, spirits that speak

or won't, souls of the dead, shades
of the blood, this or that or
something else or nothing nameable—

I stayed. I sat awake all night.
Or slept sometimes what felt like
sleep and let the void fill up
inside me, breath at a time.
By dawn, most of what had disappeared
was back again but changed. Even
the ghosts who sat with me and wept

at daylight stayed: ribbons of mist,
black branches on the ground, and
high in the trees, like nests,
spider-wire and glistening.
Now and then the spirit of a song.
Now and then the shadow of the sun,
breaking and rising. Then the sun.

Sickle

Sharper than the scythe, which, like the ladder
and the boards I couldn't lift, was long.
And quicker, since it was smaller,
and, swung in an arc, would sing.
I was the age of Latin in school, *mollis*
for mullein, the flannel of whose leaf
girls would rouge their Quaker cheeks with,
for whom vanity, even beauty, was a wildflower.
Weeds were waste, like the milkweed's semen milk,
and this was work that I could do, through
afternoons the sun would drive
your bare head into your shoulders.
Then a need for salt and the spilling
of some blood, blisters and exhaustion,
lacerate missed chances, biblical water poured—
carrot lace and goldenrod swept
to the ground like harvest, star-thorn
Canada thistle cut to the rose at the root.
I used the sickle because the scythe
was too much weight, and because death's
instrument, on the shoulder of the monk's head's
hood-and-mantle, looked too much like it.
You wanted, when you were finished, a field.

Woman on Twenty-Second Eating Berries

She's not angry exactly but all business,
eating them right off the tree, with confidence,
the kind that lets her spit out the bad ones
clear of the sidewalk into the street. It's
sunny, though who can tell what she's tasting,
rowan or one of the serviceberries—
the animal at work, so everybody,
save the traffic, keeps a distance. She's picking
clean what the birds have left, and even,
in her hurry, a few dark leaves. In the air
the dusting of exhaust that still turns pennies
green, the way the cloudy surfaces
of things obscure their differences,
like the mock orange or the apple rose that
cracks the paving stone, rooted in the plaza.
No one will say your name, and when you come to
the door no one will know you, a parable
of the afterlife on earth. Poor grapes, poor crabs,
wild black cherry trees, on which some forty-six
or so species of birds have fed, some boy's dead
weight or the tragic summer lightning killing
the seed, how boyish now that hunger
to bring those branches down to scale,
to eat of that which otherwise was waste,
how natural this woman eating berries, how alone.

Reading with the Poets

Whitman among the wounded, at the bedside,
kissing the blood off boys' faces, sometimes stilled
faces, writing their letters, writing the letters
home, saying, sometimes, the white prayers, helping,
sometimes, with the bodies or holding the bodies
down. The boy with the scar that cuts through his speech,
who's followed us here to the Elizabeth
Zane Memorial and Cemetery, wants
to speak nevertheless on the Civil War's
stone-scarred rows of dead and the battle here
just outside of Wheeling equal in death to
Gettysburg because no doctor between the war
and Pittsburgh was possible.

                                    Boys dressed like men
and men would gangrene first before the shock of
the saw and scalpel. Three days between this part
of the Ohio River and Pittsburgh. He
knows, he is here since then a child of history
and knows Elizabeth Zane saved all she could.
Keats all his wounded life wanted to be a healer,
which he was, once at his mother's bedside, failed,
once at his brother's, failed. Whitman in Washington
failed: how many nights on the watch and it broke
him, all those broken boys, all those bodies blessed
into the abyss. Now the poem for Lincoln,
now the boy with the scar almost singing, now
the oldest surviving poet of the war
reading one good line, then another, then
the song of the hermit thrush from the ground cover.
Lincoln's long black brooding body sailed in a train,

filling and unfilling the trees, a man's slow
running. Whitman had nowhere to go, so I
leave thee lilac with heart-shaped leaves, he says at
last, and went to the other side with the corpses,
myriads of them, soldiers' white skeletons,
far enough into the heart of the flower
that none of them suffered, none of them grieved, though
the living had built whole cities around them.

Keats at his medical lectures drew flowers.
Not from indifference, not from his elegance:
his interest couldn't bear the remarkable
screams of the demonstrations. He sat there, still
a boy, already broken, looking into the living
body, listening to the arias of the spirit
climbing. So the boy at the graves of the Union
singing, saying his vision, seeing the bodies
broken into the ground. Now the poem for Lincoln.
Now the oldest surviving poet still alive
weaving with the audience that gossamer,
that thread of the thing we find in the voice again.
Now in the night our faces kissed by the healer.

Will Work for Food

1

He was off the road on the island, the
handmade sign held up for recognition,
his hard face starved around his commitment
to hard work or a handout, staring straight
as a prophet, the slow summer traffic
gliding to the corner, looking, gliding,
as if he were part of an accident,
the lost parent, unnatural, or part
of another thing, a richer flowering,
and we were the poor in spirit passing.

2

Job saying, Thou my God are cruel and cast
me down to be lifted up like driftwood
on a wave, like ash above the burning
of my body, where my bones are starlight
in the cold night air, a night cloud drifting. . . .
Do I not grieve the poor on either side,
on the right and the left, did I not grieve?
I know thou will bring me into the house
to let me mourn, let me stand up ignored,
letting me cry in the congregation.

3

The flowering at the end of the long stem
of the tension, the way the mallow rose
seems nervous in its stasis, taller than
a man, common, pale, mucilaginous,
the kind of study we will wade out to

just to touch and then be disappointed
in its color, texture, odor, this wild-
flower of the destitute who cut up
flowers for flavor and want for everything
except spirit, solitude, and famine.

4

Job saying, I am driven forth by thieves
who dwell in cliffs, in caves, among the rocks
and nettles where they gather in mock prayer
to mock me as their byword and their song,
who mar my path and set my calumny,
who come upon me as a wide breaking
rolling-in of waters, wind and terrors,
a desolation and my soul poured out,
so even garments of my body change,
brother to dragons, companion to owls.

Snipers

The owls are impossible, priceless,
a hundred points at least. They live at night
and call from the dark like children.
Their heart-shaped faces, their mothlike silences.
But the carrion crows are obvious.
They enter the pines with parts of their wings
still caught in sunlight. Four, then five
of them bitching, ragging the emptiness.
Something in the wind and they last
a moment, heavy but flawless. Followed
by the jays, just as painful and skillful.
Jay-jay kee-yeeer kee-yeeer, jay-jay kee-yeeer.
One boy the first week bagged six crows' heads,
endless mice and rat tails, bodies of birds
too small to cut, a possum, whole,
and plumages of squirrels. . . .
He brought his gun to show and tell
its tunnel barrel, its abstract accuracy.
The gun said jays were quick, too beautiful,
the owls, in their Indian headdress, invisible.
It said that only the crows wear crowns
and sit in the gunsights of the trees' silhouettes
dancing but not moving. Redwings, mockers,
and the oriole were songbirds by comparison.
Another boy, at fifty points apiece,
tried to pass off starlings' heads for crows',
diminutive, yellow-billed, and dull.
He was the fool. I fooled and aimed at the trees.
The idea was to kill them back to the first crow,
the ghost crow made out of cloud,
to alter their next future.

The idea was arithmetic and order.
I remember that future now, the sixty
or so subspecies of sparrow
and the dead black weight of the burlap
doubled and dragged. The schoolroom
stank and the floor was slick with sawdust,
the iron lung and the slaughterhouse
the other long field trips that year.
At the window the rain-black light of a storm.
He said he wanted to shoot their eyes out or blow them
into the wind—kingdom come, that was the phrase,
as if the crows could care, being spiritual or suicidal,
here in the afterlife of memory and unaccountable crows,
where we'll never kill them all, nor see an owl.

Souls of Suicides as Birds

Because of his fierce red-orange hair,
which he hated and threatened to dye,
and did, on more than one occasion,
leaving the half-look of his head
strangely mottled, as if he had survived
scarlet fever, which, in his embarrassment,
he sometimes claimed he had, and because
he spoke and acted with a certain insect
abruptness yet showiness in spite of his
childish size, more diminutive each year,
and because Timothy is a grass, Tim the
diminution, he's become an American Redstart,
demonstrative at the tiptop of branches,
che-wee, che-wee, che-wee. Linda Mannus,
whose intelligent, high-wire crisis voice
piqued everyone's angst, even at twelve,
is a Chipping Sparrow, heard as well in
the backyard as among the orchard cages.
She took poison, then a razor, then ran—
Timothy Cotrell used all twenty gauges
of his gun. The farmer Elifritz drove
his tractor through a worn-out wall
of his barn, thereby piercing his throat
with old wood, and therefore is a warbler,
Black-throated Blue, who loves the swampy
interior, the dense scrub undergrowth.
Jack Butz, whose Vietnam wound was total,
like a lightning scar, lived for as long
as is possible in Piqua, Ohio, and be alive;
and Jerry Hart, star athlete, died of AIDS:
one is a Purple, one a Boat-tailed Grackle.

And when Raymond Baker flew with his Ford
Fairlane through the barrels and signs of
detour, planing his head through the wind-
shield, he became a Swift, able to dive
down chimneys and vector a straight line
of the invisible air like an arrow aimed
at silence. And the two sisters, Alma and
Kay, each impregnated by their father,
transpired for a while as Whippoorwills,
then Doves, but found real joy as Thrushes,
hermetic, unadorned, but adored at evening.
Kay found Alma hanging and followed. . . .
These friends from school—and there are more,
doubtless, I don't know about and others,
almost subtle, who crafted deaths too natural,
none of whom made it out of their thirties
or forties, none of them murdered, none
of them victims of street fire or planes,
sticks and stones or drugs, none of them missing
persons, all of them Starlings or the Siren
noise high in the Tulip Poplars. . . .

Conan Doyle's Copper Beeches

In the story they're in a clump at the front
hall door, as huge as an extinction,
yet Holmes, the literalist, ignores them,
focused on the options of the case.

It's Watson, his Boswell and naturalist,
who makes them beautiful, if only for
a moment, "shining like burnished metal
in the light of the setting sun"—Watson,

soldier, biographer of adventure.
The woman, Miss Hunter, is alone and
will be saved by deduction, then action,
and always the same conclusion—the lives

that were interrupted will go on, lives
that were broken will heal or go under,
like all the other stories an elegy
of the century, the country, the seasons.

The beeches, though hardly mentioned, suggest
the melancholy of the piece, the weather,
mood, the sense of failure in the house—
they're like a background for the color of

the clues: bright blue dress, copper coil of hair,
the bone-white starving of the dog. They
link the past, medieval to the modern,
the leaves still dark in summer, bronze and

butter through hundreds of falls and winters.
They're what's left of a larger thing. Watson
knows this, accepts his friend's insulting him
as one for whom the art is for his sake,

who loves embellishment, the odd detail,
Miss Hunter's face flecked "like a plover's egg,"
who's disappointed such a beauty will
be dropped back into private life as just

another aspect of the landscape,
one on whom nothing once was lost—Watson
the memorist Watson the lover,
writing from the heart, aware that his friend

is isolated, suicidal, bored,
perfectionist, misogynist, genius
of the obvious, a man made of glass.
The beeches turning in the wind are glass.

As for the evil parents now children
of their servants, as for the prisoner daughter
now free to marry, gone to Mauritius,
as for Miss Violet Hunter, gentle, gone—

Watson understands the resolution,
how the gray cathedral ruminating
trees display their power within a human
emptiness, letting a few leaves fall.

Humility Elm

Growing up I never thought of it by name
nor thought of it at all till it began to die,
though even that took time, slow meditating time,
in which the seasons failed, as always, to arrive
except in fragments, moments, snow piled up on rain,
summer like a drill, each oblong-ovate leaf

passed back to dust or worse, to new leaves
pockmarked, paper-dry. And death too had no name,
save that it fell as acid as black rain
into the fountain branches, then cell by cell, like dye,
down through the mile of root only to arrive
over and over. It seemed lifetime

enough to watch the elm disintegrate like time,
bark and brick, stick and stone, dead leaf on leaf,
in dehydrated colors of departure and arrival,
ulmus anonymous, until it lost whatever name
it had: *americana, hollandica, rubra, etcetera,* which die
to make the memory green against the rain—

as green as from the heartwood cut from rain
to make a bowl, the one Milton says the poetry of time
must drink from, lest the work, like the wood, die.
When my mother died her deathbed was a leaf
dropped in the water in the well of rings and names
shaped like the tower of a tree where to arrive

is to return. How she hated that elm. Autumn would arrive
and already, throughout summer, intermittent rain
of pale and broken leaves and name-

less broken branches had spoiled seasons out of time,
the roof and rough-cut corners widowing in leaf
the house she had grown up in that would die.

In the end the elm survived affection's anger to die
by force of nature, fungus, moral failure, however we arrive
at such distinctions, while dead skin spotted like a leaf
long suffering. What looked like winter rain
and winter trees were elms all year, one at a time,
and this one ours, timeless, rooted without name.

Once upon a time cattle grazed the lower, greener leaves
and men made plows and coffins out of elms—fire for the rain—
and we arrived and died within our names buried inside wood.

For My Father, Dead at Fifty-six, on My Fifty-sixth Birthday

I watched you humble a man in a fight once—
he went down like an animal whose spirit
    world has suddenly collapsed and all that's left
in the wounded moment after is not quite
    animal nor man. He was big, which made
his humility that much larger, and there
    was blood but so little that it seemed less like
a fight than a conversion. You had his right
    arm at the wrist in your right hand and simply
turned him down onto the floor, which stank of wear
    and sawdust. I'd seen you break the back of wood
like that. The man wept, he was drunk, you were drunk
    and at the same time sober. He was my size
now. And in his eyes I could see his children.

I think you turned me down like that once too, but
it was play, and then you lifted me at the
    wrist like a doll and swung me onto your back
as if I were the live weight and balancing
    you needed. And I'm remembering the time
you hammered home the forelocked skulls of steers
    whose sickness wouldn't cure—they were yours to kill
against the slaughterhousing autopsies of
    medicine—you the dire sentimentalist
who wouldn't let the dead hands of the doctor
    inside you, while all four chambers of your heart
filled with effluvium of both our lifetimes.
    The man at the bar had the option at least
of rising and changing back into a man.

Dove

Shapes as a series of edges, each edge
a wave exhausted yet extended just
enough until the shoulder is complete,
or the leaf or the chair, which is flying,
which, if we weren't flying too, we could see—
it is a beautiful shoulder, either
elegant or useful, like a calla
lily or cello or a mountain road,
it is a big, flat-handed, star-point oak,
and a rocker, elder, utterly still.
Shapes as the sunlight serial in light,
the sadness of the blur in the picture,
bend of the wing, the white wing bars, white
edges that at any distance become
integral to the losses of objects
wasting into the air like grain above
the harvest, like the close-up once I saw
of the type hitting the paper like a
hammer, exploding on the high desert
proving ground of the page in such a way
that dust along the outline of the ink
rose in a shadow of fine dead powder.
The way touching would be fingerprinted
if the flesh could somehow hold the fracture.
Waves of heat, waves of the river rising
from the river, the rainbow edges like
those lines in earth drawn with sticks that will be
straight but not in this life, love, nor money.

Dwarf with Violin, Government Center Station

The long-distance connections fade and rectify
like wind tracking the filaments of wire
through the echo of the tunnel,
the emptiness and silence pushed on up
ahead of the great green toy trains rattling
and grinding to their stops, so that the notes
have to rise even higher, toward ignition,
as electric as the switches, at a line
above the static, except they don't.
They coil and ravel out like thought.

The violin is almost the size
of the man, and graduates the longer
it is listened to, as the woman in
blankets will hear it whole through the heroin
and chill. It is a moment meant to
make us forget the moment, since the soul
wants a pastoral, a green tree on a hill:
it will close its eyes in the cave of winds
and pick the human sound, however flawed;
in the deathless weather of the understructure,

among the dead who travel underground,
it will be appalled, appeased, and then
the longing, then the coming up for air
to a sort of spring in winter, early
blossoming, yellow in the aisles around
the Common, snow-scar and construction.
The friend I saw broken, leaning against
a building, was no one I knew. I had a noise
like music in my head. Everything took heart.
Everything looked alive as if forgotten.

Alms

The woman in my building who skips
each perpendicular is a water bug,
weightless in her ability to lift
and fall lightly, ever afraid
she'll break her mother's back,
though if the reading of faces
has any value she has. Her friend
is thirty and touches every line
she crosses in her step-and-a-half
steps since her stroke, as if
she'd been struck on her whole
left side by lightning: she fades
in and out of talking and lets
the man she lives with—twice
her size and boiled at birth
in anger—speak for her. Then
there are those at the elevator
less obvious, bent internally
as by some soulful choice, sworn,
like most of us, to keep it secret.
But the woman with her head
confessionally down, who dances
over lines, and her friend
with the long gray scar, who has
half a body, have no choice—
one the leaper, the other a kind
of leper—moving in their theater
across the lobby. In a strange
city by a stranger river once,
balanced above the Isola Tiberina,
two gypsy women tried to rob me—

they were girls and one of them
was pregnant: they came straight
at me singing in their language,
pointing all their fingers at
their mouths, pouring their hands
through my poor tourist's pockets.
It happened in a moment that took
hours. Then they ran.

Keats in Burns Country

It isn't so much that Burns, like the best,
dies young, nor that he's buried among
Lowlanders, at the Borders, nor that in
eighteen-eighteen, Scotland, in spite of its
beauty, is black granite country, nor that
the Kirk is presbyterian stone
over the soul, nor that the poverty
of the dirt farmer, which Burns was and was
poorly, is medieval, nor even that
his widow survives and haunts the churchyard—
it isn't these hostilities nor those
you can imagine so much as the fact
of Burns alive in failure, with only
words on paper to compensate his death.

Tom is alive in Hampstead hanging on,
younger than both of you will ever be
again. Scotland's your epic journey
to the clouds and to the pillars under
them, yet mostly it's been a ragtag walk
between the towns' consumptive rain and chil-
blain wind, summer but an hour's paly gleam.
You think that Burns's white marble tomb's on scale
though nothing of the spirit of the man
nor the half perfect heartbreak of the poems.
You write two cottage sonnets on the spot,
the first for Tom, the second for yourself,
one at the grave, the other at the house
Burns was born in—you can't make your mind up

how you feel and what is true. All is cold
Beauty, pain is never done: then you toast
to Burns your own frail mortal body and
the thousand days you say you still have left.
This is your first warm taste of whiskey, your
first real taste of the barley-bree of fame.
Outside the birthplace windows the bright fields
run to yellow then to shade then open
north to the bedrock-covering of mountains.
Burns worked and walked here, you are thinking,
and talked with Bitches and drank with Blackguards,
the intimate sublime of what he wrote.
You're failing too and by the time you climb
the snow cloud of Ben Nevis you'll be dead.

Shadower

They were being led—though not so much led
as ushered—by a boy allowed to take
the least interest, who, when called on, made sure
they made their transfers, found a seat, and were
not alone too long, train to train, dressed for
appointments they'd likely have to walk to
once they arrived at Government Center
or Boylston. Clearly they were proud. The man
moved with power, the young woman he was with
a grace behind him, yet anyone could see
her nerves. He sometimes took her hand. The boy,
the sighted one, would go ahead or trail,
the figure or angel who disappears.

And now, thinking back, it's easy to be
struck by the healed half-closure of the eyes
and the slight tilts of their heads toward hearing,
when it was the two of them together
that gave the moment what it had, the way
they followed you, the way you followed them,
separate, intimate, sexual, as if
wherever they were going would be longing
satisfied. Someone in the blindness of
your heart was missing. The couple must have
known that you were there, like the boy, who saw
but didn't say a word, then disappeared,
as they did, once you turned your head and thought.

Panegyric for Gee

The anachronistic face of the bulldog,
the anachronistic, Churchillian face of the bulldog,
the anachronistic, Churchillian, gargoylean
face of the bulldog, the anachronistic, Churchillian,
gargoylean, Quasimodian face of the bulldog,
whose ears are silk purses,
whose eyes, like a bullfrog's, enlarge,
whose flat black wet gorilla's nose sucks the air
out of the dust, whose mouth is as wide
as a channel cat's feeding for years in solitude
on the bottom, whose two lower utter canines
show one at a time, bite that is worse than its bark,
whose slobber is the drool of herbivores,
whose brooding pose is the seal's,
who climbs and descends, who stands, who climbs again,
who at the top of the stairs in the morning dark
is beef-faced drowsy as the mastiff god—
the andiron-large front legs welded like doorstops to the
                paws—
who peers down from prehistory over the edge.
O gnomic skin and bone too big for a soul
squeezed from a root-slip in the earth,
O antediluvian noises in the throat,
O silences of staring straight ahead,
O dog-trot, O dreams of the chase ten yards and then a
                rest—.
To sleep by a bulldog is to return to the primal nasal
sleep of the drunk, the drunk whose carnal snore self-purifies
the breath with the sanctity of opera,
the rich deep long great breath of the animal beached but
                flying.

When my father slept he slept the sleep of a drunk
who'd have loved this bulldog, so stubborn at the forehead,
so set on plowing through to the conclusion of a door
too thick to pass, except in spirit,
whose singing sober voice alone breaks hearts.

One-Legged Wooden Redwing

Whittled to size and military dress,
      epaulets, eyeless, and so much
at attention sunlight is its ornament,
     this one from an island still visible
from shore, the kind of place that disappears
     in glare, the kind of light real redwings love
cutting across the level of the eyes,
     a signal of a gunfire in the blood
that startles the heart then dives,
     but this one like a blackbird in a book,
look-alike, useless as an arrow on a table,
     always alone, always the male display—
tee-err, check, check, tee-err or the liquid
     silver gurgling *konk-la-ree, o-ka-lay*—

when in fact they are gregarious
      and travel and brood at dusk
anonymous with all the other birds that feed
     above the fields and in the orchards
or forage at the shoulder of the road,
     though only the redwings are also marsh birds,
sometimes thrushes, calling from the edges,
     riding the cattails, tipping the ends of
the river branches, and only the redwings,
      of all the blackbirds, bring to the landlocked
sailor his good luck—blood on the wing, wounds
     taken up—luck to the soldiers wading
through smoke where bullets pass like rain
      against the leaves and die into the woods,

where Grant is turning redwings out of pine,
     sitting outside his white tent
writing orders to his generals in clear
   Victorian prose, for which he will be
famous beyond failure, having just returned
     to camp after a morning's ride behind the lines
looking for breakthroughs, breakthroughs now
   punched out to the other side of the air
where the ghosts among the trees conduct
their different war—their Shiloh or Cold
Harbor—and Grant is waiting for some word
   or signal back from those alive
or those who will be dead, with a little
     whiskey, stub cigar, and small pieces of wood.

The Art of Poetry

No apologies, no explanations,
a few words strung together on a line,
a tolerance of inches off the wave,
a radio wave, invisible though
audible, like a lake held in the hand,
the bright stone skipping the surface gone home.
There is so much silence in a childhood
everything is sound, everything else
an octave kicked above it, the subject
whatever in the moment comes to mind,
earth, air, fire, conversion of the water,
the half-face in the half-dark of the glass:
beyond which snow is falling, summer rain,
or the last weightless color from the leaves.

Stillness of the eye, stillness of the ovate
edge and oval window of the ear
injured into flower, rounded, poppy-red,
the blood pulled out by hand, the way the boy
Edison, it was said, had lost his hearing
and now was inward, gifted at the higher
ranges, at the stillborn singing in the light.
To travel with that voice from void to void
inside the head is to remember how
you once went down in an abstraction,
both ears boxed and blood on your hands, no one
to blame but passion, as you heard the ocean
break and give and take back what it wanted,
whose warm voice rode the water to the end.

The children who are old enough to make
live cages of their hands are handed small,
exotic birds accustomed to enclosure,
meant to be admired like objets d'art,
hand-painted out of nature, living toys,
which out of breath still panic like a pulse—
so the children hold them tighter to their ears,
who have struck their own closed eyes for color,
who see the room's gray air as a kind of
rain or braille no less real or artificial
than these yellow, blue, blue-green-yellow birds
suddenly let go, one at a time, two
at a time, for pleasure, for applause, to
watch them stutter, fly into their cages.

Bum's ears, burned black, blackhead-encrusted, rubbed
pustules: but sometimes the blood, like a nose-
bleed, cleanses, runs down the neck, like drink, or
back down the auditory canal, past
the ossicles, and, if it's bad enough,
on through the Eustachian, underground,
to pool in the throat to a hard, thick cough
caught in the mouth: the man half-drugged, half-drunk,
clubbed on the head, spilled like a pocket's contents
on the sidewalk. The blood purifies,
then corrupts. The man won't rise, is lifted
by his cuffs into the wagon's bread box,
the blood loop of the light an arc of closure,
electric as a nerve, a cynosure.

Above the thistle breaking through the stone,
high in the tulip poplars in late spring,
the fleshing-out, the first intensity

of leaves, the mocker's song divisible,
multiple, part of the weaving, part of
the light and wind, the flying back and forth
within the canopy, green on lucid
green: the song omniscient, indifferent,
whether or not anyone's there to hear it,
take it to heart. It's late afternoon,
then all at once evening: also part of
the weaving, part of the hidden branching.
Even if you care, none of it's happening
with meaning or intent unless you say.

The woman whose parents have never heard
who writes a book about it—the growing
up in silence, the reaching after speech,
the years worked out like counting on the air,
thought itself exhausting, palpable,
the mother asking once if colors make
a sound, the father incapable of
comics—who remembers being dumb in
the huge noise of school, housed with the dummies,
until her mother one day shouted no,
Rachel will speak for me, and Rachel spoke.
To throw a stone, says Darwin, is to use
the tongue, and to pick it up is to think.
How requisite these hands holding these words.

Doves in January

Long o's, long o's, long o's, and then a pause,
a whistle more like someone's voice than song,
as if in a moment a day could pass

from nothing's grief to some becoming grace.
You want to hear it longer, then it's gone.
Long o's, long o's, long o's, and then a pause.

The morning's dove-gray too; it carries us
to some deep corner, to an attic room,
as if in a moment a day could pass.

Sometimes the difficult, tired child in us
refuses to hear any other sound—
long o's, long o's, long o's, and then a pause—

a momentary wish, this tenderness
at the window, not too close but human,
as if in a moment a day could pass.

Light rain coming down the color of keys,
a daybreak's flawless stillness, cold yet warm.
Long o's, long o's, long o's, and then a pause,
as if in a moment a day could pass.

In Answer to Amy's Question What's a Pickerel

Pickerel have infinite, small bones, and skins
of glass and black ground glass, and though small for pike
are no less wall-eyed and their eyes like bone.
Are fierce for their size, and when they flare
at the surface resemble drowning birds,
the wing-slick panic of birds, but in those
seconds out of water on the line,
when their color changes and they choose for life,
will try to cut you and take part of your hand
back with them. And yet they open like hands,
the sweet white meat more delicate in oil,
to be eaten off the fire when the sun
is level with the lake, the wind calm,
the air ice-blue, blue-black, and flecked with rain.

Lazarus at Dawn

Your whole life you are two with one taken
away. The inadequate air and fire,
the inadequate joy, the darknesses
of the room so gathered at the window
as to fly, wing on wing on wing open
against the glass, opening and closing,
bone, blood and wrist. But nothing happens but
exhaustion and evidence of the eyes,
the red-gold cloud-break morning beginning

with the objects that floated in the dark
draining back to the source, floating back to
the surface tension of things, those objects
struck the way the first light starts suddenly,
then slowly in relief across the room,
the window's shadow garden come back one
last time once more from the leaves. Waking now,
the door half-open, open, the doorway's
blindness or blackness silence to be filled.

A man was sick, a sickness unto death.
All he wanted to do was to lie down,
let the light pick him apart like the dust.
He wrapped himself, in his mind, in his own
absence. He did not want to hear the rain,
with its meaning, nor the moment after
rain, nor the sound of Jesus weeping, nor
the dreaming, which is memory, though he
lay a long time cold, head against the stone.

You see the wind passing from tree to tree,
thousands of green individual leaves
silver and fluid at the surfaces,
the long nothing narrative of the wind.
The wind is the emptiness and fullness
in one breath, and the holding of that breath,
restlessness and stillness of the spirit.
You see your dead face in the gray glass close,
and see that it is already too late,

that death's blood nakedness clothed white is smoke,
the father standing in the doorway white,
whom you see in part, the way the morning
gathering is part in the slow degrees
of rectitude, a kind of twilight dawn.
Nothing is said, though he knows you love him.
Nothing is said, though you know he loves you.
Longing, as a sickness of the heart, is
invisible, incurable, endless.

The Last Parent

Of course she'll wave good-bye, the ocean liner's
melancholy size towering like Manhattan.
Of course she'll be obscure standing at the rail,
the only visible passenger, like someone
at a window so small she disappears
behind the beauty of her gesture,
her raised hand one of the waves that starts
at sea and builds. And later on of course
she'll stroll the high elliptic of the deck
while each immortal hour plows the colder,
deeper shades toward where the sun perpetually
sets its billion bullion lode and lays a gold
path leading west, easy to follow, within
whose wake, against the dark, this sail.

Drunks

In 1948, when I was nine years old, I helped my father build a house—the house I lived in for the next ten years and where my mother and he lived until he was fired from his foreman's job at the French Oil Milling Machine Company for being late to work a hundred too many times. We'd moved from Virginia and the Shenandoah Valley the year before. My father and grandfather had had a falling-out, which can happen when a son works for his father. So we moved to my mother's town, on the western side of Ohio, where postwar industries were just starting up. The idea of buying land and building on it was inspired by the housing project we'd had to settle in since there was nowhere else in a city crowded with new jobs and opportunities. It was called Victory Heights, was barrackslike and a natural for returning Second World War veterans, of which my father was none. How we managed to get into the place I'm not sure, but we were there more than a year, on Nimitz Court, while the house in the country was taking shape. All the streets in Victory Heights were named for admirals or generals. The road where our house would be was named after a horse breeder who lived nearby. I remember how much better that suited me. Later, my first girlfriend was this horse dealer's daughter. Everything seemed new and sort of made up on the spot after the war, so it wasn't surprising that streets and roads should be named after people still alive. Perhaps it gave them something to live up to. Garbry Road began at the city limits and ambled a couple of miles or so toward a larger road. It was really a country lane. Our property was about halfway between town and where the road ended. We dug the foundation in the spring, near my birthday; we also dug holes for a row of maple trees, meant to celebrate my birthday—and also, I think, to inspire me to a greater work ethic during the hot summer months and cold winter months it would take to finish the house. Enough to say about the house that my father built it virtually by himself with his own two hands; making something, it seemed to my young eyes, from nothing; creating order out of a chaos of bricks and boards, sawing and nailing. I carried things, mixed things, messed up things, asked a thousand questions, and generally kept my father company. I turned nine when we started and ten when we more or less finished, though the house, as a perfect construct, was never quite finished. My father worked on it the way some people write books, after work. He was thirty-three and putting in sixteen-seventeen-hour days. After a while it may have been psychologically impossible for him to finish the house, just as it was psychically impossible for my mother not to complain. Anyway, the house went up. I remember one early March day, nearly a year into its building, when it was still depressingly cold and snowy and windy and there was yet no roof, I remember sitting at the edge of what would be my bedroom looking up at the dead white sky thinking nothing else could be this empty. Nothing else could be or feel this erased, as if a cold stone in the chest had suddenly melted into the bloodstream. In the middle of the open space of the house my father had placed an oil drum and started a fire. All winter he'd started a fire. But this particular day, with spring promised by the end of the month and the fire climbing into the air, the hopelessness of ever getting shelter over our heads strangely and suddenly combined with a touch of euphoria in my mind and I felt lifted: I thought what a great thing not to have to have a roof and to live under the sky. I felt watched and oddly cared for and knew that if I fell asleep among these walls that were like ruins I could be picked like an apple from the floor. The hand that does these things could just make me disappear. The snow-blind sky. I learned to drink around that oil-barrel fire. It was that watery beer made in Cincinnati. By the end of the day, my father would have drunk himself dumb, usually with the help of a little whiskey to build heat under the beer. I could barely down a bottle. We'd drive back to Victory Heights drunk. It would be a long time into the future before I ever felt unsafe in my father's company, whether he was at the wheel or not, though I wasn't with him when he wrecked the new car.

It was a '48 Chevy Coupe, maroon, a month old, and sleek, as if the paint were still wet. He'd won the car in a raffle at the local movie theater. You got tickets for the raffle by buying goods from the town's merchants. Building a house meant a lot of purchases. Half the tickets must have been his. My mother and he were returning from a party in Dayton and he ran a light. The accident totaled the car, but they walked away without a wound. The alcohol must have saved them. My impression is that if you can stop drinking before you're forty you have a chance. My father was drunk every day of his life, except for a few Sundays. It's not surprising that he couldn't quite complete the house; or, as he aged past forty, get to his job on time. He was a kind of failed house himself—large, complicated, incomplete. The summer we moved into the Garbry Road house he and I drove up to Canada to fish. It was meant to be the reward for a job well done. Just the two of us. I remember we fished a big lake, as all lakes seem to be once you're on them, and it was deep and clear and black cold, somewhere in Ontario. We pulled in a muskie and a great deal of pickerel. We were out on the water most of the day. The big northerns would float up under the boat, take a look and pass under—they were hard to catch and mean. The boat was like a small room in a house, the cab of his truck, and every closed-in space my father dwelt in. It had booze in it. The second evening on the lake my father stood up drunk and began to rock. It was a dance, pathetic yet magical. I knew we would never turn over.

The Marriage in the Trees

When the wind was right everything else
was wrong, like the oak we thought built
better than the house split like a ship
on rock. We let it stand the winter,
spectral, shagged, every sky its snow,
then cut it down, dismantled it in
pieces like disease. Then limbs from
the yellow poplar broke at will—
fell from the heights like bones
of the Puritans; even to gather them
in bundles seemed puritanical.
And the willow, by its nature, wept
long tears of its overbranching,
so pale they were autumnal. These
we turned too easily to switches,
mocking the bickering in the spruce's
nesting eaves, which crows, then jays
bothered all they could. The list,
the list. The sycamore made maps
of disappearance; the copper beech,
parental in its girth, was clipped
hard, by a car, with a wound that wouldn't
heal. Doctoring, then witchery, then
love—nothing we tried would work.
More apple trees that grew nowhere
but down. More maples spilling sugar.
More hawthorns blazing out, telling truth.

Nobody Sleeps

One theory is that acid wastes in the blood
accumulate and depress the brain so much
it wants to lie down at the mouth of a cave
on a high hard ledge shelving over nothing.
It wants to think of nothing, be nothing,
and wake up empty with sleep in its eyes.
Another is that during waking the brain
uses up its oxygen faster than the body
can replace and is so starved by the end
of the day it seeks a bed of branching
in order to lay its head on laurel green.
And a third says that because the afferent
impulses of the neurons are contractile
with the dendritic process of the cells
any interruption over time isolates
the cortex from external stimuli and
as interruptions peak in sync with dark
the brain wants to lie all night by fire.
The theory of anemia, involving the loss
of tone in the vascular heart of the medulla,
is too particular, especially since,
except in fits and starts, nobody sleeps—
though there are children who sleep through
anything, even memory and waking, and adults
who work the night shift or the street
who only pretend by closing their eyes,
even in daylight. But the vertical brain
wants to lie down, beside water if it can
or under wind topping the tall pale grasses.
It wants to alter its relation to the bed
to give up gravity to the ground, to let

the mind float out in spirit-buoyant air,
to feel, at the foliate edge, the mind
relieved. And because it cannot sleep
it wants to dream the sexual narrative
of longing and connection, the journey
of the body in light continually dying,
the cold wet morning air silvering down
on the night earth warming toward the sun,
and then to hear the first bell-clarity of song,
which, if you were dreaming, would wake you.

Cardinals in a Shower at Union Square

At first they look like any other birds
on gun line from the underbrush, so someone
calls them sparrows and someone who thinks
he knows, scarlet tanagers or something else
exotic, as if they've slipped captivity—
one of those white sky August days the hammer
of the heat picks out the old one or the child
locked in a car, while gathered above the blank
grave of the pavement, at the altitude of snow,
enough rain to almost forgive it all.
Only two are really red, the rest a buoyant
dried blood brown, young or female, all of them
with masks and crests that make them what
they are, explosions from the other side
or blown in, with the paper, with the storm.
Whoever starts the clapping is answered
by a show of hands to meet baptismal waters
and a couple, who are high, bird-dancing.
Whoever starts the shouting is quieted
by the lady who hears silences,
cupping her clownish ears. . . .
For a moment the ringing air is clean, then
for a moment nothing happens, nothing moves
except the cardinals, in and out of trees.
And in that moment ends. The cloudburst
passes, the air turns into fire again,
the sirens sing their distances, the walls
of light burn down. And in no time,
in the time it takes the runoff to drain

back underground, there's no one left
but lifers and the dealers and rain birds
swallowed upward by the sun, and rain, new rain,
in the rivers and the reservoir uptown,
ready to rise and pour its heart out all over.

Detail Waiting for a Train

The main floor of Penn Station, early,
the first commuters arriving, leaving,
the man outstretched on his coat,
wide circles of survivors forming.

He's half in, half out of his clothes,
being kissed and cardio-shocked,
though he was likely dead before he landed.

This goes on for minutes, minutes more,
until the medics unhook the vanished heart,
move him onto the cot and cover him
with the snow-depth of a sheet

and wheel him the fluorescent length
of the hall through gray freight doors
that open on their own and close at will.

Field

In ornithology there occurs the phrase *the abrupt edge,* which, according to the bird books, is "the edge between two types of vegetation . . . where the advantages of both are most convenient." In the less precipitous sense such edges are gradual, over a distance, sometimes up to miles, where a woodland thins out to shrub and grassland or a hedgerow drifts into ellipsis and disuse and finally pasture. In the more abrupt forest-at-the-edge-of-the-field sense, however, trees will stand isolated in a grove, in open country, or clumped in a thicket by a good river, like islands; closer to home, the protective hedge and shrub corners of a garden will act as a border, while the line of young maples or the understory of pyracantha and azalea will mark the boundary between safety and vulnerability. The advantage of the edge is that it allows the bird to live in two worlds at once, and the more abrupt the more intense the advantage. From a position of height or secrecy, the bird can spy for danger or prey; it can come and go quickly, like a thief. Where the vegetation is more varied, the shade and cover thicker, the insect life rising, the tanager can sweep down from its treetop, the thrush can fly out from the gloom, and the redwing can sit the fence post all day in the summer sun. The edge is the concept of the doorway, shadow and light, inside and outside, room and warlde's room, where the density and variety of the plants that love the sun and the open air yield to the darker, greener, cooler interior world, at the margin. It is no surprise, then, that the greatest number of species as well as individuals live at the edge and fly the pathways and corridors and trails at the joining of the juxtaposition. That is where the richness is, the thick, deep vegetable life—a wall of life, where the trees turn to meadows, the meadows to columnar, watchtower trees. A man of sense, coming to a clearing, a great open space, will always wait among the trees, in the doorway, until the coast is clear.

Farragut North

In the tunnel light at the top of the station two or three
figures huddled under tarps built against the wind crossing
Connecticut at K. It'll be noon before they rise in their
Navajo blankets, trinkets, ski masks and gloves to start
the day, noon before the oil slicks of ice on the sidewalks thaw.
—In the forties, after the war, in the Land of Uz, when
somebody came to the house for a handout, my mother'd give
him milk money or bread money as well as bread and milk.
To her each day was the thirties. The men at the door had
the hard-boiled faces of veterans, soldiers of the enemy.
My mother saw something in them, homelessness the condition
of some happiness, as if in the faces of these drifters could be
read pieces of parts of herself still missing: like the Indian
woman in Whitman's *Sleepers* who comes to his mother's door
looking for work when there is no work yet is set by the fire
and fed: so that for my mother, the first time she left,
it became a question of whom to identify with most,
the wanderer or the welcomer.—The stunted sycamores on K are
terminal, though they'll outlast the hairline fractures marbling
the gravestones of the buildings. Under the perfect pavement
of the sky the figures frozen in this landscape contemplate
the verities too fundamentally for city or country: their isolation
is complete, like the dead or gods. When I think of a day with
nothing in it, a string of such days, I think of the gray life of
buildings, of walking out of my life in a direction just
invented, or, since some of us survive within the mental wards
of our own third worlds, I see myself disguised for constant
winter, withdrawn into the inability to act on the least impulse
save anger and hear myself in street-talk talking street-time.
—Such is the freedom of transformation, letting the deep
voice climb on its own; such is the shell of the body broken,
falling away like money's new clothes; such is my mother's
truant spirit, moving dead leaves with the wind among shadows. . . .

Complaint Against the Arsonist

This pyrrhic fire the barn burned down and blew back
into the dust-weight of its carbon, that burned the air
flecked bright with it, above the wheat in flags,
the barn I spent the summer part-time painting, white
on white to purify the wood, the summer I wheeled ashes
in a foundry, working the aisles between castings
and the cutting edge of molds, ashes I had to hose down hard
like a dog pile of the intimate earth transformed. . . .
At night my arms would levitate like wings, a diamond
in each hand, the morning sun a low round furnace gold.

In those eighteenth-century English paintings alchemizing
ore, the ones with the dawnlike sunset reds and yellows
always rising, the silhouettes of buildings rising behind
the fires, the foundries are invisible, nothing but storms
the rain-gray horses are pulling the wagons from,
the night shifts ending, the pitch-black skies poised
like the weight of history above a pastoral—before Turner
and Constable and the oxygen conversion of the landscape
into light—when the picture is still the reality of record,
heightened for effect, named for Coalbrookdale or Bedlam.

That night was industrial and animal, a burning-off of flesh,
the blue clouds' upward drifting like the longing of all
          clouds—
you had to stand there hours thinking what it was like,
this dying-off, this earth-transcending gift, the mind a
kind of angel sent ahead, since the suicide is to set the fire
and stay, to let it pull you in, like falling or flying,
since the men I worked among, the one who stayed,

had seen in fire what fire can do, if not this soaring
of a wind straight up, a living building all at once,
the blood screams breaking like electric lights

around the horse that came out stumbling, then soared.

William Matthews's Armistice Poppies

Lucky elevens, Saturday, November,
the marching band and veterans in regalia,
the chipped chrome Cadillacs, cannons strapped to trucks,
the rest of us left buttonholed on corners,
children and parents in every baseline color,
the poppies' stiff cheap crepe running in the rain. . . .
Why is it always raining?
I look up into the cold clouds blinded,
opening my hands, my cat's-mouth yawn a poppy.
The rain has the taste of ice, it kills
things down to an essential clarity—.

2

Poppies everywhere, horizon to some middle distance,
against the summer yellow of the grain,
in sunlight so bright it burns a violet ash
at their centers, the petals tucked and scored,
their soft blood orange ecstatic rose
wounded at the stem. To pick
them is to have them close and dry up into leaves.
Better to let them labor on their own,
solitary, terminal, open above the field,
the disc-shaped cups arrayed yet tipped
among the broken pottery of the wind.

3

In the park across the street
the widow wearing medals from the First World War
sorting with her cane daffodil from crocus.
She pokes at them as if to count them.

This, like every other, is her fatal spring.
And this the year we leave the windows open,
London ocean air alternately heavy, lambent, falling,
the nineteenth-century plane trees
transitional between purple and the foliation,
the new grass wet with ice and fuel exhaust,
each lily of a flower once touched dismissed.

4

The subject is debility, the wind against the house,
the spirits at the table arguing
happiness, survival, the middle of the night,
and how the next-door neighbor,
who's finished out the war in German boxcars,
sometimes walks the outline of his yard,
then lies down face up to the few visible stars.
His body has no floor. Except for his name
it's understood he disappears in daylight,
except for the dark he's anyone's
silence, absence, father.

5

Midsummer, south of Edinburgh, cool, the evening
fine and pale, the North Sea cumulus clouds
moving among the farms at galleon speed.
Under the weight of light the poppies spread out evenly,
while opposite the road the big white Grays
browse above their shadows and drift awhile
before they lean against the fence to bob for apples,
which eaten whole break in half and flower.
Someone who hates his life stands in the road,
on one side the dark red distance of the poppies,
on the other side great souls.

Constable's Clouds for Keats

They come in off the sea peaceable masters
and hold the sea in the sky as long as they can.
And you write them down in oils because of their
brilliance, and to remember, in its turn, each one.

It's eighteen twenty-two after the Regency,
and it would be right in the year after his death
to think of these—domed above the Heath
in their isolated chronicle—as elegies

of the spirit; right to see these forms
as melancholy hosts, even at this distance.
Yet dead Keats is amorphous, a shapelessness
re-forming in the ground, and no one you know enough

to remember. He lies in the artist's paradise
in Rome, among the pagan souls of sheep at pasture.
You'll lie in Hampstead where he should have stayed
to meet you on your walks up Lower Terrace

or along the crowning High Street heading home.
Your clouds grow whiter, darker, more abstract
from one elaborate study to the next,
correlatives, or close, to the real sentiment

that lives, you say, in clouds . . . subjects to counter-
weigh the airy gravity of trees and leaping horses.
Keats could have met you—you must have seen him once
against the light, at least. He could be

crossing on Christchurch Hill Road now, then
over to the Elm Row and down Old Admiral's Walk.

He could be looking at the clouds blooming between
buildings, watching the phantoms levitating stone.

He was there your first Heath summer writing odes,
feeling the weather change from warm to chill,
focused, no less than you, on daylight's last detail,
wondering what our feelings are without us.

Hedgerows

How many names. Some trouble
or other would take me outside
up the town's soft hill, into the country,
on the road between them.
The haw, the interlocking bramble, the thorn,
head-high, higher, a corridor, black windows.
And everywhere the smell of sanicle
and tansy, the taste
of the judas elder, and somewhere
the weaver thrush that here they call mistle,
as in evergreen, because of the berries.
I'd walk in the evening,
into the sun, the blue air almost cold,
wind like traffic, the paper flowering of the ox-eye
and the campion still white,
still lit, like spring.
I'd walk until my mind cleared,
with the clarity of morning, the dew transparent
to the green, even here, in another
country, in the dark,
the hedgework building and weaving
and building under both great wings of the night.
I'd have walked to the top of the next
hill, and the next, the stars,
like town lights, coming on,
the next town either Ash Mill or Rose Ash.
Then sometimes a car, sometimes a bird, a magpie,
gliding. This is voicelessness,
the still breath easing.
I think, for a moment, I wanted to die,
and that somehow the tangle

and bramble, the branch and flowering of the hedge
would take me in, torn, rendered down
to the apple or the red wound or the balm,
the green man, leaf and shred.
I think I wanted the richness, the thickness,
the whole dumb life gone to seed,
and the work to follow, the hedger with his tools,
ethering and cutting, wood and mind.
And later, in this life,
to come back as a pail made of elm
or broom straw of broom or the heartwood of the yew
for the bow, oak for the plow—
the bowl on the wild cherry of the table for the boy
who sits there, having come from the field
with his family, half hungry, half cold,
one more day of the harvest accounted,
yellowing, winnowing,
the boy lost in the thought
of the turning of the year and the dead father.

Analogies of the Leaf

Almost dark, late spring. And nothing in the chances
of the visible, first stars but a hunter and a ram
and women so virginal they give off fire
to light the pathway up the ladder to the stair—
nothing in the columnar night wind
but the hollowing of air,
the whistle empty at the tag end of the song.
Along the back, along the rainbow
vertebra, at the spear point of the spine,
my hand cuts like a leaf. You turn and open,
as my mouth opens over yours.
When I enter you your face takes on
the focus of a thought suddenly
appropriate to how your knees have worked
up under my arms, your eyes shutting on the sources.
Then the blurred, spilled shape of the willow
finding water, letting its low branching down.

When the wind blows back against the leaves
they turn a kind of silver, like fish,
we said as kids, and rubbed them raw to watch
the flash and glitter come off clean in our soiled hands.
It never did, though we said it did.
And the rain that can turn leaves silver, quick as mercury—
something else for the hands to fail to catch.
The evening is scaled and set, counting blue
and blue and blue, the way a petal
or a stone is stained. You come down flushed,
then white and cool. The story of the body
is endless interiority,

following or not following the blood
back to the glassy breath—sympathetic
pathways, arterial, vaginal, thecal—
the spirit passed between us, mouth on mouth,
the soul so rooted in the other it is flesh.

Against Starlings

1

Their song is almost painful the way it
penetrates the air—above the haze and
level of the fields a thin line drawn. A
wire. Where the birdcall goes to ground. But I'd
stand anyway under the oaks lining
the road and whistle, tireless with chances,
tossing, by the handful, the crushed stone.
All of them answered, none of them came down.
By evening there'd be hundreds filling the
trees past hearing, black along the branches.
They'd go off with the guns like buckshot, black,
filling the sky, falling. I held my ears.
The holes in the air closed quickly, then healed.
Birds were bloodless, like smoke, wind in a field—

2

But not to be confused with the cowbird,
its brown head, its conical sparrow's bill,
nor with the redwing, which is obvious,
even showy, blood or birthmark, nor with
the boat-tailed grackle—though at dusk, when they
gathered from the north, they were all blackbirds.
They were what the night brought, and the blown leaves,
and the cloud come down in the rain. The ease
of it, the way summer would be ending.
When I found one one morning it was the
color of oil in a pool of water,
bronze, blue-green, still shining. The parts that were
missing were throwaway, breast and belly
and the small ink and eye-ring of the eye—

3

Not to be compared with the last native
wild pigeon, trap-shot high in Pike County,
Ohio, the fourth day of spring, nineteen
hundred—thirty years after the harvest
of millions filled the buffalo trains east.
They were, by report, "the most numerous
bird ever to exist on earth," what the
Narragansett called Wuskowhan, the blue
dove, the wanderer, whose flight is silent.
Not to be compared with the smaller, wild
mourning dove, which haunted the afternoon,
which you heard all day till dark. They
were the sound in my sleep those long naps home,
the last train calling down the line in time—

4

Sometimes, at the far end of a pasture,
the burdock and buckwheat thick as the grass
along the hedgework, you could still find nests,
some fallen, some you had to climb to. They
were a kind of evidence, a kind of
science, sticks, straw, and brilliant bits of glass.
My mother had a hat like that, feathered,
flawed—she'd bought it used. It was intricate
and jeweled, the feathers scuffed like a jay's,
and so stiff you could've carried water.
The millinery species is over.
Those nests had nothing in them. Still, sometimes
I'd wait until the autumn light was gone,
the sky half eggshell, half a starling's wing—

5

Not to be compared with the fluted voice,
the five phrases in different pitches
of the thrush, the one Whitman heard, and Keats,
Sturnus vulgaris vulgaris—not to
be confused with the soft talk and music,
the voice that calls the spirit from the wood.
Those that stayed the winter sat the chimney
to keep warm, and cried down the snow to fly
against the cold. They were impossible.
They'd be dead before spring, or disappear
into the white air.—Not to be confused
with the black leaves whirling up the windward
side of the house, caught in the chimney smoke,
the higher the more invisible—

6

                    Black.
I saw them cover the sky over a
building once, and storm an alley. They were
a gathering, whole. Yet on the window-
sill, individual, stealing the grain
I put there, they'd almost look at me through
the glass. Something magical, practical.
They'd even graze the ground for what had dropped.
I wished for one to come into the house,
and left the window open just enough.
None ever did. That was another year.
What is to be feared is emptiness and
nothing to fill it. I threw a stone or
I didn't throw a stone is one language–
the vowel is a small leaf on the tongue.

Cedar Waxwing on Scarlet Firethorn

To start again with something beautiful,
and natural, the waxwing first on one
foot, then the other, holding the berry
against the moment like a drop of blood—
redwing-tipped, yellow at the tip of the
tail, the head sleek, crested, fin or arrow,
turning now, swallowing. Or any bird
that turns, as by instruction, its small, dark
head, disinterested, toward the future; flies
into the massive tangle of the trees, slick.
The visual glide of the detail blurs.

The good gun flowering in the mouth is done,
like swallowing the sword or eating fire,
the carnival trick we could take back if
we wanted. When I was told suicide
meant the soul stayed with the body locked in
the ground I knew it was wrong, that each bird
could be any one in the afterlife,
alive, on wing. Like this one, which lets its
thin lisp of a song go out into
the future, then follows, into the wood-
land understory, into its voice, gone.

But to look down the long shaft of the air,
the whole healing silence of the air, fire
and thorn, where we want to be, on the edge
of the advantage, the abrupt green edge
between the flowering pyracantha and
the winded, open field, before the trees—
to be alive in secret, this is what

we wanted, and here, as when we die what
lives is fluted on the air—a whistle,
then the wing—even our desire to die,
to swallow fire, disappear, be nothing.

The body fills with light, and in the mind
the white oak of the table, the ladder
stiffness of the chair, the dried-out paper
on the wall fly back into the vein and
branching of the leaf—flare like the waxwings,
whose moment seems to fill the scarlet hedge.
From the window, at a distance, just more
trees against the sky, and in the distance
after that everything is possible.
We are in a room with all the loved ones,
who, when they answer, have the power of song.

The Wyoming Poetry Circuit

Climbing down out of the rain, which is what
the breakable upper branches were: rain:
webbed, hardly visible vessels, the imprint
of the leaves long since Cambrian, Ordovician,
rooted out of time, the cold breakable
rain branching out of sight, but thicker
the lower down you went, thickest at the trunk. . . .

My father had put me up there to look
for deer, above the scent. I never got
it right—it all looked rain to me,
the star-points at a distance blurring
with the trees. Two other moments: one
with friends in a great field in the spring,
the cold sky filled or emptied out of wind,

the Steller's jays angry or friendly depending,
then suddenly a redwing flies into
my hand just long enough to take the bread.
I can see the spots, like a starling's,
and the clipped, blood reds lit within the wing–
it is amazing, a moment, and nothing.
And the other: above the Wind River

Basin, in moon country, along the skyline,
the loose trail of antelope drifting
with the herds—heraldic, half wild, following
the traffic down to better pasture,
dead meat and following to slaughter.
We have to stop the truck to let them pass:
they congregate in front of us, like cages.

Light then dusk passes through them. Wyoming
is dusk, all day—I remember it seemed
deeper in the air, layers of the inter-
tonguing rock permeable, passable, like rain,
like a storm in daylight passing to the north,
the Indian towns starving with the dark,
the ranches poor with oil or coal or the

animal debt of the land, which had a shine
like dry seabeds or maria, silver,
though they held their shadow. In Sheridan
we met in a hunting lodge to talk,
no one from anywhere you could name,
who loved the place or got stuck—we talked into
the night, the still walls lined with signs and wonders.

Love will never let us alone, which is
exactly what it does. That night it got
too late. Even outside, in moonlight,
we could see our faces, people you'd never
see again, who'd traveled hundreds of miles
in a landscape through stone just to talk
or hear the poem read against silence.

The next morning was winter, the rain
ice cold, October, but by afternoon
clear with the smell of snow. All those towns to
get through, all that endless gradual ground.
At Wind River the walls were stratified,
like ladder variations on the color
stone, a ladder to be dreamed of climbing

• • •

from the earth—we stopped to watch the river move
its tons of trainloads of the rock. My friend
said that stone is what they have instead of
trees, which are immortal, flowering out of
stone like souls in secret. I could believe
it, counting the outcrop few leading toward
the horizon. The small stone in the hand,

she said, is for loneliness, company,
good luck. To the south, past Rawlins, there were
elk, like shale and mud and blue dusk, part of a cut
that had climbed out of the river: animals
part tree, part stone, coming down, she said,
to feed with the herds, to take a look at us,
but not too close, or close, or not at all.

Toward Umbria

It isn't the poppies,
their red and accidental numbers,
nor the birdfoot-violets, their blue lines
wasted, nor the sheer, uninterrupted
wayside pastures—nor along the river
the centuries-faded terra-cotta farmhouses,
outbuildings, floatings of iron, iron windmills,
                              pastoral or neutral,
like the ancient towns walled-up in sunlight
and the failed machinery left abandoned.
From a summer I can still see the sidewalk
broken by a root and follow, in a thought,
the bull-blue thistle wild along the fence wire
into the country. Here the thistle blooms

too tall, the color of clover, Great Marsh and Musk,
and spiked like roses. Something about its
conference and size, its spine indifference—.
                              We are drift and flotsam,
though sometimes when we stop to look out over
the landscape, outcrops of limestone and a few
stone sheep, the ground itself seems torn,
and when we drive along the white glide of the river,
the high wheat grass like water in the wind,
someone in joy running from the house,
the story is already breaking down.
The season is ending, fire on the wing,
or the season is starting endlessly again,
sedge and woodrush and yellow chamomile,

anywhere a field is like a wall, lapsed, fallow
or filled, a stain of wildflowers or a wave
of light washing over stone, everything in time,

                       and all the same—
if I pick this poppy, as I used to
pull up weeds, wild strawberries, anything,
a city will be built, we'll have to live there,
we'll have to leave. Once, and in one direction only.
And the figure on the landscape coming toward us
will be someone we knew and almost loved, or loved,
for whom this moment is equally awkward,
as for those ahead of us it is equally condemned,
plowmen and gleaners, shepherds-of-the-keep,

                   those on the road, those lost.

Birthday

An old mortality, these evening doorways into rooms,
this door from the kitchen and there's the yard,
the grass not cut and filled with sweetness,
and in the thorn the summer wounding of the sun.

And locked in the shade the dove calling down.

The glare's a little blinding still but only
for the moment of surprise, like suddenly
coming into a hall with a window at the end,

the light stacked up like scaffolding. I am
that boy again my father told not to look
at the ground so much looking at the ground.

I am the animal touched on the forehead, charmed.

In the sky the silver maple like rain in a cloud
we've tied: and I see myself walking from what looks like
a classroom, the floor waxed white, into my father's
arms, who lifts me, like a discovery, out of this life.

Cloud Building

All night there'd have been
an anger in the air, terror of voices, threats,
   the argument half dreamt, then calm,
      then the hard doors shutting
   into sleep and cold and waking with the sun.
I'd have risen for school and made a hole
    in the window ice to see through:
     blown piles of the inches
   of the snow, and in between, like ponds,
the blue-brittle surfaces with a high blue
   cirrus shine, exactitude of color
    in the eye. Even the brightness
  and shape of the smoke coming
from the chimney were divinations of the wind,
    the body broadcast, the winter leaf let go.
     Say a bird had hit the glass,
   first light, like a snowball with a stone,
tossed at remarkable distance.
  At the cool heights of the mind
    it should have been a cardinal
  or a jay, something with color,
something to see instead of a piece of something,
    nothing but gray ice stony broken.
     And now it comes in a dish,
   in the new year, melted white
as albumen, as water in a bowl, or else so dry
  you could blow it back to crystal.
    It comes back now in the least
  disguise as paper and ash,
the day's first fire falling back on the house
    in a story with the wind, a ragtag

starling, or crying, the snowy
   light crazy with perfection.
You hold a thing just dead it will burn
     in your hand like a lie told to the body.
       You hold someone in your arms,
    the cloud of sperm still drifting like a spirit,
you think she'll disappear, the heart
    immaculate. The cold radiance–
     it wants a white light dry as dust
     in the eye; it wants to leave
the body through the mouth and come back slowly,
   pure with patience, shine slowly
      as something else we'll never know
  except alone, like the sentimental
old, who are full of stories,
    or children, who in solitude have silence.

Infidelity

The two-toned Olds swinging sideways out of
the drive, the bone-white gravel kicked up in
a shot, my mother in the death seat half
out the door, the door half shut—she's being
pushed or wants to jump, I don't remember.
The Olds is two kinds of green, hand-painted,
and blows black smoke like a coal-oil fire. I'm
stunned and feel a wind, like a machine, pass
through me, through my heart and mouth; I'm standing
in a field not fifty feet away, the
wheel of the wind closing the distance.
Then suddenly the car stops and my mother
falls with nothing, nothing to break the fall. . . .

One of those moments we give too much to,
like the moment of acknowledgment of
betrayal, when the one who's faithless has
nothing more to say and the silence is
terrifying since you must choose between
one or the other emptiness. I know
my mother's face was covered black with blood
and that when she rose she too said nothing.
Language is a darkness pulled out of us.
But I screamed that day she was almost killed,
whether I wept or ran or threw a stone,
or stood stone-still, choosing at last between
parents, one of whom was driving away.

Above Barnesville

In the body the night sky in ascension—
the starry campion, the mallow rose, the wild potato vine.
You could pick them, though they'd die in your hand.
It's here, in the thirties, that the fathers panned for gold,
pick-and-shovel, five-to-a-dollar-a-day—you could survive
panning the glacial drift, the split rock, the old alluvial scar.
If you climb the brick path back to the top of the hill,
for the long hard look, you can still see Quaker poverty,
the sheer tilt of the green-gray roll of the land,
the rock-soil thinning out, the coal breaking ground like ice.
Some of the farmers still use horses for fear of the height, the
      weight against them,
as all the working day you can walk to the abrupt edge
of property and watch machines opening the earth.
The valley, the locals call it,
a landscape so deadly the water pools to oil before it clears—
a kind of kerosene, a few dropped stars or sunlight.

Deep autumnal nights I imagine my parents lying side
by side on the good grass looking up at the coal-and-diamond dark,
as they will lie together for the rest of their lives.
The star lanes scatter, and disappear. I will be born
under the sign of the twins less than a mile from here,
with too much blood on the floor. My father, right now,
is turning toward my mother. In the doctrine of signatures
the body is divisible, the heart the leaf of a redbud
or the blue ash in a fire, the genitalia
the various and soft centers of the shell
or the long spathe and cleft, the pink pouch of the flower.
They will be waking soon.
Overhead the chill and endless pastoral of the sky, the
      constellations drifting.

For a moment the mirror is laid beside us—Cassiopeia, Ursa
Minor, the Plow—parts of the house, a door left open, a window,
so that we can see how far down into the earth the path is leading.

The word for wood is xylem, which is the living tissue,
and by a kind of poetry graduates inward
from summer to winter to sapwood to the heart.
I was with my father the day he found
the tree that had been gouged and rendered useless and cut down.
It was probably hickory or walnut, black, the dull bark split
and furrowed, like a field: it seemed a hundred feet,
most of it in branches, the feathering of leaves turning color at
        the top.
The size of it, so suddenly alone.
My father, in his anger, cut away until the wood was soft. . . .
In the rain the smell of tannin, fire and char, poignant on the air.
I remember how thin the upper branches were, intricate as nests,
how impossible to climb this high without falling, breaking through.
It seemed to have come down from the sky in stages—
the broken branches first, then the medulla and the root,
then, deep inside, the lumber flying at the brain.

At night, sometimes, you could hear the second shift,
and fantasize the train's elliptical passage through the town
or the mythical ocean pulling moonlight from your windows.
You could hear the celestial traffic taking off.
But in the morning, crack-white and plain, it would be nothing
but the earth made new again, a little less each time.
Once, one of those pure October days that seem to rise,
I came up over the scab-hill of a mine—all slag and oxidation,
the sick ground running orange in a stream, here and there
the skeletons of buildings. It looked like parts of a great abandoned
        house

ruined in a fire in the middle of a woods saved by snow.
It had seasons, memory—
nothing like the Dipper-sized machines
digging into the hillsides by the houseful.
A month ago I could have picked wildflowers, corn-blues and
    goldenrod,
while in the summer I'd have never found the place in so much
    green.

In the constellation named for the bottles tossed to the side of the
    road,
for the poverty of leaves blowing one-way down the lane,
for the stones flecked like fish, for the water carried with both hands
    closed,
the stars are of the sixth and seventh magnitude.
You can hardly see them in the broken glass and the ash from the
    burn-off.
In the coal-colored dark it's all pinholes and candles,
and this is as close as we'll ever get,
as when we close our eyes something gossamer like nebula floats up.
I told my father not to die, but he didn't listen.
He got down on his knees as if to hold on to the earth,
as if to hide inside his body.
In the black and crystalline light of coal and rock,
through the flake and mica leaves, layer upon layer,
he would not climb the ladder so loved by believers.
For that I love him, and find him safe
in the least of things alive—dust on the road, wind at its back.

Those first cold nights you could taste the ice in the air.
North seemed to mean the stars, where the snow came from.
Even now you could see it start to fall. Sides of the trees white
with it, heelprints and tire tracks white with it,

the little edges of the roofs, like the drawing in the kitchen, white
  with it.
If we could make it cold enough and snow enough, such silence!
Even now, with color in the leaves, you could almost see it falling.
My mother called it the ocean, the way it covered everything,
the way in the morning the light of it was blinding.
She'd watch it for hours, letting it fall.
I think of her following my father as if by a miracle of leverage,
the one pulling the other out to sea. I think of how I will follow her,
how she brought me here, half her body, half of the rest of her.
Those nights the constellation shapes glistened into water
I thought it was forever, I thought it was enough,
though I knew that if water rises stones will burn.

Pityriasis Rosacea

We say the blood rose, meaning it came to the surface
like a bruise, which comes from outside, blue, in a small violence,
a stone, a brush against the table, the punishment of riches;
or meaning the deep object, the blood rose, which is artifice,
since in nature what to look for is color neutral, mallow,
a little pale, like florals years on the canvas, themselves
a kind of nature now with the light and dust in the room's
atmosphere; or meaning the viral air picked out this blood
to rise like the rash after sex, which darkly pollinates
the skin, delicate, in a rush of the blood returning, like
a weight of ash, to the heart, except that here it comes
in petal-, sepal-sized extrusions, but softer, like embarrassment,
the flaw a fire-leak in the blood, hectic, risen, flush
on the upper body with passion, intermission, mouth of the kiss.

The sickle, the scythe in the blood, which means to sweep
the tide of its impurities, like a sword in the wave, cuts, fails,
rises like a thorn—we say this too is the blood burning clean.
But only the wren flower, yarrow, or the nettle will heal the old
wound or the dry bleeding, which made the flesh blush even to itself
and the boy on the hillside, working in a fever of the summer
against the wire of undergrowth, walk away, because his hands
wouldn't close. The raw rose on the back of my hand is a sign
of the season, something in the air, like pollen and the garden
phlox we let grow wild, sick purple, pink, what a child or a man
might worry meant corruption of the purest part, the blood,
which is immortal and fire on the river running backward, forward
in a wind, dangerous, anonymous as any other part of ourselves
passed on, scattered, or poured back into the earth.

The Foundry Garden

Myths of the landscape—
the sun going down in the mouths of the furnaces,
the fires banked and cooling, ticking into dark, here and there the
      sudden flaring into roses,
then the light across the long factory of the field, the split and rusted
      castings,
across the low slant tin roofs of the buildings, across fallow and tar
      and burnt potato ground. . . .
Everything a little still on fire, in sunlight, then smoke, then cinder,
then the milling back to earth, rich earth, the silica of ash.
The times I can taste the iron in the air, the gray wash like exhaust,
      smell the burn-off,
my eyes begin to tear, and I'm leaning against a wall, short of breath,
my heart as large as my father's, alone in such poverty my body scars
      the light.
Arable fields, waste and stony places, waysides—
the day he got the job at the Wellbaum and Company Foundry he
      wept,
and later, in the truck, pulled the plug on a bottle.
In the metallurgy of ore and coal and limestone, in the conversion of
      the green world to gray,
in the face of the blue-white fire, I remember the fencerow, the white
      campion,
calyx and coronal scales, the hawthorns, cut to the size of hedge,
the haws so deep in the blood of the season they bled.
The year we were poor enough to dig potatoes we had to drive there,
then wait for the men to leave who let the fires go out.
There'd be one good hour of daylight, the rough straight rows running
      into shade.
We'd work the ground until the sun was a single line.

I can see my father, now cut in half by the horizon, coming toward
    me, both arms weighted down.
I can see him bending over, gone.
Later, in the summer, I'd have painted the dead rust undulant sides
    of all the buildings aluminum,
which in the morning threw a glare like water on the garden.

Men Working on Wings

In dreams they were everything hurt
whose faces were always coming into focus
like a feeling never before realized
offered now as longing; but not spiritual,
like the cloud in marble or the flaws
in sunlight streaking through the window,
but palpable, the way that cloud,
those flaws take on the human.

If I have to choose I choose those nights
I sat in the dark in the Mote Park
outfield waiting with my father
for the long fly balls that fell more
rarely than the stars. We'd talk
or he'd hit the hole in his glove;
a hundred times he'd hit the hole
in his glove. In his factory wool-

and-cotton gray uniform he looked
like a soldier too young to fight,
like his sailor brother and our monkey
uncle doughboy Harry who'd been gassed
in the trenches—too young to fight.
But nobody died. Once, on the Ponte
S. Angelo, leading from the Castle
of Angels across a wrist of the Tiber,

I watched the artisans of the working
classes work with the patience of repairmen
on the backs of the immortelles. Except
for their hands they sat the wings

in stillness, hammer and chisel, like
any other sculptors; the job endless,
infinitesimal, a constancy of detail,
the air itself the enemy, and the long

gold light pouring down. The big flat
dead leaves of the sycamores would whirl
around them in a theme, then drift
like paper to the river. The leaves
might float, in another life, all the way
to the sea, spotted and brown like the backs
of the hands of the old. The wings
of the angels were stone clouds stained,

pocked like a bird's. My father didn't want
to die, nor my uncles, in their fifties,
nor dull Jack Bruning, who'd have welded
wings to his back to get another day
of drinking, and who claimed that
in the war he'd eaten a man's flesh.
At one another's funerals they were
inconsolable: they would draw from

the scabbard, with its lime-green rust,
a sword against their deaths; in their
flawed hearts they would stand fast:
as on the bridge, with half-closed eyes
and mouths about to speak, the ten
Bernini angels, in their cold and heavy robes,
and wings unfurled with the weight of men,
were in alignment yet reluctant to cross.

Fountain Park

At a hundred feet or more the maples
and the oaks are another architecture
building on this life the gold leaf of the next,
scattered in sequence, linked like windbreak.
No matter how miraculous the stiff
flight of the fish or the balance of gifted
children on their toes, no matter that the god
has drawn his sword against his nakedness
and the lily is a girl closed against the cold,
I can't remember when the fountains worked,
spread like all the other cemetery
sculpture into a city in a valley,
here and there the graveyard grass like pasture.

From the top of the hill it's Saturday,
empty, early in the evening, in season,
the sun in detail now, a kind of tone,
a kind of candlepower the wind could easily
blow out, the way it kindles the dry leaves
in the bowls of the fountains—pillars of
fire, water from a stone. In the bridgework
of the leaves I'm holding, the nine-lobed oak,
the compound willow feather, all kinds of things
pass witness and are true about this last
light of the day coming onto winter,
the trees almost transparent in their dark,
the high grass green as lawns in the hereafter.

With Stephen in Maine

The huge mammalian rocks in front of the lawn,
domestic between the grass and the low tide—
Stephen has set his boat in one of the pools,
his hand the little god that makes it move.
It is cold, the sky the rough wool and gabardine
of pictures someone almost talented has painted.
Off and on the sun, then Stephen is wading. . . .

Yesterday we saw two gulls shot out of the sky.
One of them drifted into shore, broken, half eaten,
green with the sea. When I found it this morning
all I could think to do was throw it back. One wing.
Its thin blood spread enough that Stephen is finger-
printed and painted with washing and wiping dry.
Even his boat, at the watermark, is stained.

I lift him, put him up on top of my shoulders.
From here he can watch the deep water pile, turn over.
He says, with wonder, that it looks like the ocean
killing itself. He wants to throw stones, he wants
to see how far his boat can sail, will float.
The mile or more from here to there is an order of color,
pitched white and black and dove- or green-gray, blue,

but far and hurt from where he is seeing.

Four Appaloosas

First the glycerin, green transparency of rain,
the stations of the air shifting around them, in columns,
like the trees, next to which they stand in a kind
of pattern, even the one at the fence watching the traffic,
all of them stained like stone, mud and gray and pearl,
backs to the wind. Then the gulls coming down,
like lights, out of a cloud . . . ice white.
The sea is yoked but huge against the ground, tidal
in its weather, only miles from here. You feel its weight
in the shapes of things, antipodal, bent-nail,
the scarring of the branches black and lateral,
the rain suddenly visible at angles mixed with snow.
Now the shorebirds are the knocked-off hats of the horses. . . .
Now the snow sticking white to the windshield.

Early and Late in the Month

<u>1   *Paddington Recreation Ground*</u>

White birds on the cold green winter grass, wet
with white, like snow held too long in the hand,
the runner's white breath ghosting the gray air.
The morning is one thing, then another—
rain, sometimes the sun slick along the trees,
sometimes the sudden thought of clouds settling
for the day, then lifting. While I slept none
of this was here, none of this drifting, though

I remember in the evening I watched
the sky hurt with the blue at the cold quick
of all color, then grow dark, and darker,
infinitely. The day moon held the moon.
I watched sunlight, hard against the windows,
disappear, watched the brickwork leave the dull-
red row of buildings, watched the street turn black
and electric, and finally oil with ice.

I woke up cold, like a boy late for school,
the photographic air granular, alive,
then lay almost an hour sorting nothing
from nothing, waiting for the room to fill.
Outside, in the half-rain, half-snow, half snow
themselves, the birds had gathered from the tide.
The man on the track was running away,
dressed in the cold colors of the morning.

<u>2   *First Day of Spring*</u>

All afternoon the industrial light
of London dissolving into rain, the

106

sexual, interminable patchwork
of the plane trees piling in perspective.
Silver and copper, like money in the
street, brilliant through the large upper window.
My eye, hooked like a bird's, fixes on any-
thing, even in memory: how the black rain
washes clean, how the dry leaf opens and
is lifted whole back into the new wind.
The spirit puts its nose against the glass—
the sky is nothing, is a starved black wing.
Below: the mirror tops of cars, the warped
iron railing the kids will try to tightwalk.

The James Wright
Annual Festival

That night we flew into Pittsburgh where Tom Flynn met the plane to drive us back to Ohio just over the river into Belmont Count where we were to meet Galway and the hosts of the Second Annual James Wright Festival for supper and the chatter of a late night before the first day of readings. What I remember from the long ride in from the airport—a new spring night with constellations broken and the blurred edges of the foothills building against the wind in a wall up from the river—is the dark and how it came into the car at a speed we understood, how it filled in the small lights going out everywhere behind us, how it moved on our faces; how later, after dinner, all of us tiring, it touched all our faces. What I remember from Galway's face that night is how the next day he talked about the work, up until the end, on the last book, or didn't talk but got lost in the moment of the last poem of *that Vence morning many times since,* and how he waited there, in thought, with the many sources. On the Sunday I spent the empty early morning wandering too, lost in Martins Ferry, where down the street from the library the Heslop Brothers were still in business and farther still the WPA Swimming Pool Project plaque shone like a war memorial object. And I walked down to the water, the beautiful Ohio, Depression-wide all the way to Wheeling, and saw that whatever the working terrors are they are worse over there, on the other side, laid off, sabbath or dead-time on the line, where hell is still a foundry and a glassworks and an icehouse filled with coal, where they take you, out of pity, in the morning before daylight and bring you back in the evening, fire in the sun, white-of-the-eye-of-the-moon; and that even the petty farmers, our fathers, had come down from the farms to cross. James Wright, Galway would finally say, had gone to the end of the table, which we will earn, as we earn the daily bread set before us, and in Galway's face, in the room of the gathered that day, you could see the winter daybreak poem take form, in a whole other country, in high gold Mediterranean air but lifted here like stone or lumber flat above the river.

Coming into La Guardia
Late at Night

The glide almost outside of time, the plane
at landing speed. It's January, dead
clear as starlight, the city in the air,
the Manichean pitch-black of the buildings
six thousand feet up the window mountain.
Adrift and north: Capella, Canis Minor.
In another year, leaving the city
in a car, I could see in the mirror
from the backbone of the bridge the wet sun
sliding into just one building, gold on
gold, and into the shadow wells. Like those
blossoms that fall to earth from light-years off,
some of the fire stays, some floats like torches
passed ahead of us along the pathways.

Boy on the Step

He's out of breath only halfway up the hill,
which is brickwalk, awkward, and just steep enough
his mother's letting him rest but all the while
coaxing—there's like a climber's rope gone slack
between them, the thing you trip when your eye goes
from her face to his and then his arm, the left
one, off at the elbow, wrapped in heavy gauze.
This is none of your business yet intimate,
the way surprise is open, vulnerable,
the way the woman who came up to you was
anyone, pretty, so innocent of guile
you thought she was lost until she got too close
and the child in her turned hard, scared, her hand thrust
out for change, anything, wounds in the air, rest.

2

Gray forest earths. Across the street from the Church
of Pilgrims, Taras Shevchenko is alone
with his audience, who understand bondage
and the freedom of the street. He's a genius
of the independent life of the spirit
and speaks in poetry—they answer him in
lines that cut into the marble at his feet,
as those in love or angry mark a tree. The
broken glass and beer cans celebrate the space
of this island whose height is statuary,
stationary in the human. With distance
you can watch at night the match-fires, hear the sounds
of the small talk of exile, witness, transience,
articulate, American, close to ground.

3

Once, in a foreign city I knew, I was
lost, really lost. Nights running I slept outside—
days I'd walk astonished, ten miles, more, then circle.
The loneliness was like belief in something,
like carrying a nail tight inside the hand.
There was blood in my shoe, I could taste its salt
like sweetness in my mouth. And the windows were
tireless, and the worn maps of stone. One long night
outside Victoria Station I sat with
those for whom nothing's forsworn, all forsaken.
They tipped their bottles the way they held hands,
to keep out the cold and only to connect.
If they were lost they'd thought the heart of it through
enough to commiserate, curse loss, and piss.

4

A prophecy of mist—it came in October
in the morning up from the river and the
rail yard, from smoke of the low fires banked inside
the yellow and the red trees, smoke like steam from
the work trains, stalled, waiting to be loaded, smoke
that rising early with the whistle you could
float out into, like sending forth the spirit.
I see those train lights now coming in, in fog,
or car lights passing with men going off to work,
the business of the night still left inside the
business of the day: that rain like silk still
holding. Things in such light are fragmentary,
cold, and reconnected later in forms we
might not recognize as friendly or history.

5

None of us dies entirely—some of us, all
of us sometimes come back sapling, seedling, cell,
like second growth, slowly, imperceptibly,
in the imprint of rings that wind like music
written down, in notes and bars, scale and silence.
Even the child, who was immortal, becomes
purity, anonymity inside us.
Which is why to watch a tree turn into fire
or fall is like a second death, like the grace
in stillness gone, exploded, fatal, final,
as someone loved, within whose face we confused
the infinite with the intimate, is last
a name, the point of a green leaf drawn across
the heart, whose loss is felt, though invisible.

6

The way the elms die is autumnal, yellow,
defoliate, long years in death, though the wound
is superficial since the heart- and sapwood
are already dead—you could find it with a
pocketknife, as if it were mold and natural.
These were wonderful, their famous fountain branch-
ing pendulous, both sides of the street, medieval,
tall as the cold ceilings in churches, endless
with extinction. Stephen, who is nine and would
need a ladder just to reach the least first branch,
can't believe they're gone, because he's heard of them
and sees them everywhere in other trees, as
if a tree could haunt a tree, like the Horace
Webster elm, which survives by luck of science.

7

Nineteen forty-five—whipsaws, handsaws, wedges
and hammers, half the men handicapped or old.
They seem old. Yet they take down the trees with care,
let them break and overlap on the whole street,
everything in sight domestic or half wild,
like countryside. It will be hours of cutting,
chain-pull and hauling before North Kent is cleared.
Later, with every other mother and child,
I'll look down into the deep well of an elm,
phloem and cambium, into the annual
rings and rays, into the pool where the leaf was
dropped, where the saws burned at angles where the rain
had poured, turned hard, into the waters of trees
where the blue stones and the white stones are a hill.

8

Wood smoke rising among hundreds, thousands
of feet of trees, the thrashers signing, counter-
signing the morning—after breakfast the crews
can cut till noon without stopping. I'm amazed
at the level of the noise, the choral sawing,
the monkey-chatter of the men, the bridgework
of branches falling. It hurts as much to hear
as see: then one of the men is falling, his
absolute voice abrupt against silence.
He's able to rise, and run, and knock me down—
he's holding out his hand, wood spikes through its palm.
He's on fire. I think I see flame on his arm.
When they catch him he's numb, already laved in
blood, blood as I've never seen, blood and sobbing.

9

To bring the hardwoods down, the maple in the
oak, the ones that split like stone, is one thing—to
bring them in is block-and-tackle and a long
ride, topped off, sheer and stacked to roll and size on
the double bed of the truck. And the ricochet
of the road doesn't help, at town or mountain
speed, the big load edging one way first, then back.
Most of the time the driver's half dead-drunk,
happy with the weight of the dead world behind
him—shifting with power, downshifting, going with
the curve, the circle inside gravity. He
understands that lumber is alive inside
the tree, that it will fly back up the mountain
in time, fly true, and at a wonderful speed.

10

What we were after was too high for a man
to reach alone, so I stood on his shoulders
and still had to climb—something left behind, some-
thing wished for, something killed. We'd already cut
the thorn and undergrowth and failed hickory trees,
this clearing with its canopy and byplay
of leaves and openness that if you stayed too
long began to bother you, as if the star-
net of sunlight had divided into nerves.
I can't remember what we were after, but
when we went there late at night, solvent, soaked to
the bone, I'd try to sit with him like a man
who knows something and who's figuring the odds
against the time, the flaws, the empty-always.

11

Sunday afternoon, a wind, leaves on the lawn
so dry they rise as if to paper the trees
again. Someone has gathered all the red ones
he can find—he's going to look at them one by
one. From the road the lawn's baronial, deep
to the Home, all the veterans dressed to order.
My mother's second father has a friend here
who's short of breath and speaks through an instrument.
They met at the Somme. The other war's won as
well, so there are younger men my father's age.
And so I'll understand I'm told they're all like
orphans, even the old ones. It's a show, a
kind of holiday, a speech—in other words
the body is a joy or it is hell—.

12

He climbed, they said, the stone ladder, and you could
see it in his face and feel it in the room—
the cloudy colors of stone, the rinsed-out, some-
thing-almost-yellow of the flowers, new, cold.
He pulled, they said, the stone bell rope of the bell
in heaven, and you could hear it the way you
sometimes hear rain on the edge of the window—
his still hands folded, holding the bell rope still.
He looked small, the navy uniform too big,
small, and wounded at the center. He slept so
well, they said, because flesh and bone are nothing,
because he was already gone to the snow
and silver palaces. But I touched him
anyway, empty, boy and body, the dream

nothing to believe, nothing like the foreign
war in which fathers were sons again, and real.
The train blew by the house filled with airplane parts
and apparatus of the shell and dead steel—
on the sides of the cars the UNITED STATES
OF AMERICA in letters large as the
windows soldiers would lean out of waving us
good-bye or windows, coming back, with small flags.
I was a child but I knew that any man
dying was a poverty and that a train
was both the thing itself and the poor memory
of the bodies brought back thousands of foreign
miles, through time and loved country and the hometowns,
to die again, with family, in hallowed ground.

14

Like an angel uncle, whose snow-white sailor
hat I floated in the bath with one of his
shoes, who'd come back from the Pole but too far
north of the war to die—unlike the angel
soldier-sailor sitting like sculpture at the
far foot of his coffin, wings enfolded, his
dark child's-head distracted . . . Those pictures they'll
have of us, in a bled-out brown and white, will
show us walking on our hands or scaling trees
or sitting on the brother step for the one still
absent, and this, with all our sun-at-the-end-of-
the-street-gone-gold-on-green melancholy, will
be the work of a god whose gift is the moment
lost or past, passed on to children of memory.

Tree Ferns

They were the local Ohio palm, tropic in the heat of trains.
They could grow in anything—pitch, whole grain,
cinders, ash and rust, the dirt
dumped back of the foundry, what

the men wore home. Little willows,
they were made to be brushed back by the traffic of boxcars
the way wind will dust the shade
of the small part of a river.—They'd

go from almost green to almost gray with each long passing,
each leaf, each branch a stain
on the winded air. They were too thin
for rain—nothing could touch them.

So we'd start with pocketknives, cutting and whittling them
     down
from willow, palm, or any other name.
They were what they looked like. Horsewhip, whipweed.
They could lay on a fine welt if you wanted.

And on a hot, dry day, July, they could all but burn.
At a certain age you try to pull all kinds of things
out of the ground, out of the loose gravel thrown by trains.

Or break off what you can and cut it clean.

After Whistler

In his portrait of Carlyle, Whistler builds
from the color out: he calls it an arrangement
in gray and black and gives it a number in order
to commit us to the composition—to the foreground
first, in profile, before we go on to a wall
that seems to be neutral but is really the weather.
Carlyle is tired, beyond anger, and beautiful,
his white head tilted slightly toward the painter.
He is wearing a long coat and rests his hat on his knees.

When I was born I came out holding my breath, blue.
The cord had somehow rotted at the navel—
I must have lain alone for hours before they would let
my father's mother, the other woman there, give blood.
She still had red hair and four years to live.
The place on my arm where they put the needles in
I call my mortality scar. When I think of my grand-
mother lifting me all the way to the kitchen counter
I think of the weight by which we are doubled or more

through the lives of others. I followed her
everywhere, or tried to. I was her witness.
When I look at Whistler's portrait of Carlyle
I think of how the old survive: we make them up.
In the vegetable garden, therefore, the sun is gold
as qualified in pictures. She is kneeling in front
of the light in such a way I can separate skin from bone.
She is an outline, planting or preparing the ground.
For all I know she will never rise from this green place.

Even the painter's mother is staring into the future,
as if her son could paint her back into her body.
I was lucky. In nineteen thirty-nine they still
believed blood was family. In a room real
with walls the color of buckwheat she would sit out
the afternoon dressed up, rocking me to sleep.
It would be Sunday, slow, no one else at home.
And I would wake that way, small in her small arms,
hers, in the calendar dark, my head against her heart.

Wildflower

Some—the ones with fish names—grow so north
they last a month, six weeks at most.
Some others, named for the fields they look like,
last longer, smaller.

And these, in particular, whether trout or corn lily,
onion or bellwort, just cut
this morning and standing open in tapwater in the kitchen,
will close with the sun.

It is June, wildflowers on the table.
They are fresh an hour ago, like sliced lemons,
with the whole day ahead of them.
They could be common mayflower lilies of the valley,

daylilies, or the clustering Canada, large, gold,
long-stemmed as pasture roses, belled out over the vase—
or maybe Solomon's seal, the petals
ranged in small toy pairs

or starry, tipped at the head like weeds.
They could be anonymous as weeds.
They are, in fact, the several names of the same thing,
lilies of the field, butter-and-eggs,

toadflax almost, the way the whites and yellows juxtapose,
and have "the look of flowers that are looked at,"
rooted as they are in water, glass and air.
I remember the summer I picked everything,

flower and wildflower, singled them out in jars
with a name attached. And when they had dried as stubborn
as paper I put them on pages and named them again.
They were all lilies, even the hyacinth,

even the great pale flower in the hand of the dead.
I picked it, kept it in the book for years
before I knew who she was,
her face lily-white, kissed and dry and cold.

In Passing

On the Canadian side, we're standing far enough away
the Falls look like photography, the roar a radio.

In the real rain, so vertical it fuses with the air,
the boat below us is starting for the caves.

Everyone on deck is dressed in black, braced for weather
and crossing against the current of the river.

They seem lost in the gorge dimensions of the place,
then, in fog, in a moment, gone.

                       In the Chekhov story,
the lovers live in a cloud, above the sheer witness of a valley.

They call it circumstance. They look up at the open wing
of the sky, or they look down into the future.

Death is a power like any other pull of the earth.
The people in the raingear with the cameras want to see it

from the inside, from behind, from the dark looking into the light.
They want to take its picture, give it size—

how much easier to get lost in the gradations of a large
and yellow leaf drifting its good-bye down one side of the gorge.

There is almost nothing that does not signal loneliness,
then loveliness, then something connecting all we will become.

All around us the luminous passage of the air,
the flat, wet gold of the leaves. I will never love you

more than at this moment, here in October,
the new rain rising slowly from the river.

Posthumous Keats

The road is so rough Severn is walking,
and every once in a while, since the season is
beautiful and there are flowers on both sides,
as if this path had just been plowed,
he picks by the handful what he can

and still keep up. Keats is in the carriage
swallowing blood and the best of the bad food.
It is early November, like summer,
honey and wheat in the last of the
daylight, and above the mountains a clear

carnelian heart line. Rome is a week
away. And Severn has started to fill
the carriage with wildflowers—rust, magenta,
marigold, and the china white of cups.
Keats is floating, his whole face luminous.

The biographer sees no glory in this,
how the living, by increments, are dead,
how they celebrate their passing half in love.
Keats, like his young companion, is alone,
among color and a long memory.

In his head he is writing a letter
about failure and money and the ten-
thousand lines that could not save his brother.
But he might as well be back at Gravesend
with the smell of the sea and cold sea rain,

waiting out the weather and the tide—
he might as well be lying in a room,
in Rome, staring at a ceiling stylized
with roses or watching outside right now
a cardinal with two footmen shooting birds.

He can still remember the meadows near
St. Cross, the taste in the air of apples,
the tower and alms-square, and the River
Itchen, all within the walk of a mile.
In the poem it is Sunday, the middle

of September, the light a gold conglomerate
of detail—"in the same way that some pictures
look warm." He has closed his eyes.
And he is going to let the day close down.
He is thinking he must learn Italian.

By the time they reach the Campagna the wind
will be blowing, the kind that begins at sea.
Severn will have climbed back in, finally a
passenger, with one more handful to add
to what is already overwhelming.

Promising the Air

A woman I loved talked in her sleep to children.
She would start her half of the conversation,
her half of asking, of answering the need to bring
the boy up the path from some dream-lake, some

wandering source, water, a river, or a road along
the tree line of a river, she would say his small name,
then silence, privacy, the drift back to the center.
The child was the tenderness in her voice.

I can remember waking myself up talking, saying nothing
that mattered but loud enough for someone else to hear.
No one was there. It was like coming alive, suddenly,
in a body. I was afraid, as in the dark we are each time

new. I was afraid, word of mouth, out of breath.
Waking is the first loneliness—
but sleep can be anything you want, the path
to the summerhouse, silence, or a call across water.

I am taught, and believe, that even in light the mind
wanders, speaks before thinking. This piece of a poem
is for her who wept without waking, who, word for word,
kept her promise to the air. And for the boy.

My Mother's Feet

How no shoe fit them,
and how she used to prop them,
having dressed for bed,
letting the fire in the coal stove blue

and blink out, falling asleep in her chair.
How she bathed and dried them, night after night,
and rubbed their soreness like an intimacy.
How she let the fire pull her soft body through them.

She was the girl who grew just standing,
the one the picture cut at the knees.
She was the girl who seemed to be dancing
out on the lawn, after supper, alone.

I have watched her climb the militant stairs
and down again, watched the ground go out from under her.
I have seen her on the edge of chances—
she fell, when she fell, like a girl.

Someone who loved her said she walked on water.
Where there is no path nor wake. As a child
I would rise in the half-dark of the house,
from a bad dream or a noisy window,

something, almost, like snow in the air,
and wander until I could find those feet, propped
and warm as a bricklayer's hands,
every step of the way shining out of them.

Sonnet

Whatever it is, however it comes, it takes time.
It can take all night.
My father would sit on the edge of the bed
and let the tears fall to the floor,
the sun the size of the window, full
and rising. He was a dead man and he knew it.

I think of him almost every time I fall in love,
how the heart is three-quarters high in the body.
—He could lift his own weight above his head.
—He could run a furrow straight by hand.
I think of him large in his dark house,
hard in thought, taking his time.

But in fact he is sitting on the edge of the bed,
and it is morning, my mother's arms around him.

Summer Celestial

At dusk I row out to what looks like light or anonymity,
too far from land to be called to, too close to be lost,
and drag oar until I can drift in and out of a circle,
the center of a circle, nothing named, nothing now to see,
the wind up a little and down, building against the air,
and listen to anything at all, bird or wind, or nothing
but the first sounds on the surface, clarifying, clear.

Once, in Canada, I saw a man stand up in his boat and pass
out dollar bills. It was summer dark. They blew down
on the lake like moonlight. Coming out of his hands
they looked like dollar bills. When I look up at the Dippers,
the whole star chart, leaves on a tree, sometimes all night,
I think about his balance over cold water, under stars,
standing in a shoe, the nets all down and gathering.

My mother still wakes crying do I think she's made of money.
—And what makes money make money make money?
I wish I could tell her how to talk herself to sleep.
I wish. She says she's afraid she won't make it back.
As in a prayer, she is more afraid of loneliness than death.
Two pennies for the eyes, two cents: I wish I could tell her
that each day the stars reorganize, each night they come back new.

Outside tonight the waters run to color with the sky.
In the old water dream you wake up in a boat, drifting out.
Everything is cold and smells of rain. Somewhere back there,
in sleep, you remember weeping. And at this moment you think
you are about to speak. But someone is holding on, hand
over hand, and someone with your voice opening and closing.
In water you think it will always be your face that floats

to the surface. Flesh is on fire under water. The nets go back
to gather and regather, and bring up stones, viridian and silver,
what falls. In the story, the three Dutch fishermen sail out
for stars, into the daylight hours, so loaded with their catch
it spills. They sleep, believe it, where they can, and dry
their nets on a full moon. For my mother, who is afraid to sleep,
for anyone afraid of heights or water, all of this is intolerable.

Look, said the wish, into your lover's face. Mine over yours.
In that other life, which I now commend to you, I have spent
the days by a house along the shore, building a boat, tying
the nets together, watching the lights go on and off on the water.
But nothing gets done, none of it ever gets finished. So I lie down
in a dream of money being passed from hand to hand in a long line.
It looks like money—or hands taking hands, being led out

to deeper water. I wake up weeping, and it is almost joy.
I go outside and the sky is sea-blue, the way the earth is looked at
from the moon. And out on the great surfaces, water is paying
back water. I know, I know this is a day and the stars reiterate,
return each loss, each witness. And that always in the room next door
someone is coughing all night or a man and a woman make love,
each body buoyed, even blessed, by what the other cannot have.

Fifth and 94th

People are standing, as if out of the rain,
holding on. For the last two blocks
the woman across the aisle has wept
quietly into her hands, the whole
of her upper body nodding, keeping time.
The bus is slow enough you can hear,
inside your head, the traffic within
traffic, like another talk.

Someone is leaning down, someone has touched
her shoulder. But by now she has tucked
her legs up under her, grief given over.
She will not lift her face.
Across the park the winter sun is perfect
behind the grill-work of the trees,
as here it is brilliant against buildings.
Above her body the thousand windows blur.

Blossom

And after a while he'd say his head was a rose,
a big beautiful rose, and he was going to blow it
all over the room, he was going to blast blood.

And after a while he'd just put his head in his one good
hand the way children do who want to go into hiding.

I still can't get the smell of smoke from the woodstove out of my head.
A woman is frying bacon and the odor is char and sour and somebody
running a finger over your tongue. All those dead years and the
    grease

still glue on the wall. In Winchester, Virginia, the year the war
ended, the blacks were still dark clouds. My uncle had a knife
pulled on him holding his nose.

                        When the Guard marched eleven
German prisoners of war down from Washington they marched them
right through town, and it was spring and a parade like apple
    blossom.
Black and white, we lined up just to watch.

I still can't get the smell of apples out of my head—
trees in orchards all over the county, like flowers in a garden.
The trees the Germans planted that spring looked like flowers,

thin as whips. Even so the branch of a full-grown apple tree
is tested every summer: when I didn't watch I picked along with
every black boy big enough to lift a bushel. Frederick County.

The National Guard in nineteen forty-five was my father and any
other son who stayed home. Next door the father of my friend
had been home two long years, one arm, one leg gone. He was

honorary. He was white sometimes, and black, depending.
He was leaf and wood smoke and leaning always into the wind.

And everybody called him Blossom because of the piece of apple
he kept tucked at the side of his mouth. When he was drinking
he'd bring his bottle over and talk to my father about Germans.

They go down, he'd say, they all go down on their guns.

Each five-petaled flower on the tree means an apple come summer.
I still can't get the bourbon smell of Blossom out of my head.
He spits his apple out and shoots himself in the mouth with his
        finger.

For Judith on Valentine's Day

1

There is the poverty of children shy with child—
the girl who will not say what is already
part of her breath, like a second wind, another mouth.
And there is the poverty of rain, in spring,
clean on the streets, the small roofs of the city.
And poverty of desire in prison hallways, cell by cell. . . .

And poverty of the wheelchair and the deathbed
and the blind who tow them where they're told.
Or flowers along the railway and the river,
poorer with every passage.

               You should look
into your hands right now—they'll hold
the poverty of grief until you let it go.

You should look into the light—it is the dust made whole.

The poverty of the bird that flies in the window
or the yard dog tied to the ground—rooms with doors
locked on the dumb who talk to themselves. . . .
These are stones that will shine.

For the poor own the houses you will not visit;
they own the trees that are dead all day.
They own the table and the chair and the glass of water.

And they let their children go hungry who will eat all the bread.
And they let their children go cold who will take what is warm.

You should look around you how the dark is poor.

And, Masters, how all this city planning comes
to one dead-end or another—block after block
abandoned, as in the loneliness after a fire.
This could be snow falling through the roof, nineteen
hundred and one, or the air that will open above Dresden.

I have seen people stunned, sitting in the center of their rooms,
watching the street like children who have sinned.
I have seen a child's shadow, the shadow of a child,
at the same sill the same each day.
And nowhere in the mind of that child

nor in what its father sees
is the shade tree rooted where the ground is green
or the wind off water and the sea rose bending.
The sad eyes looking back at me
give nothing for nothing.

And the girls, so young they still bloom toward the future
and seem almost beautiful with memory,
though we know what they long for is beyond desire,
their bodies burning even as they close,
they will be mothers, year after year,

and will sit at tables half in, half out of light,
waiting for something as at the hour assigned
in a room adjacent where they can be alone
and be at peace and let themselves lie down in a long death,
still married to need and the needs of others.

3

The round green tree—impossible to pick
the first dead leaf out of the leaves,
though it's already bright with the wound,
like the bruise on fruit or the shape of the birthmark.
This is how the young come out of the tree,
wounded, like the lyre-shaped leaves, to survive
the sadness of beginnings, to go back
into the root and branching, the perfect
longing, the desire of the heart breaking,
healing.
        The idea of winter is detail,
light in snow, the wind shining and poverty
of endings, the apple half-leaf, half-lyre.
The angel flocks are homing above builders
impossible to see, who build from inside
the wood to the green growing. Even these,
the angels, must eat of the earth to make
the difficult passage back to the everlasting.

After Rilke

American Ash

The day is late enough you could stand
within the time it takes a door to drift
back shut and watch half a tree go dark,
the other half still green with the afternoon.
I have in mind the big one down the street,
west of the house, the light so stacked and split
it bottles up, brilliant at the top.
Downing going the other way is shade.
Upstairs the light is candle-in-a-shell.
Someone is getting ready to go to bed.
The house is rich with camphor, mint, and oil
of wintergreen, and on the dining table
roses in a bowl.
                          I think it is nineteen
forty-five. Sepia will never get
quite right the year in color, my mother's
dress, for instance, red and yellow daisies
on a regimental blue to end the war,
nor my father home from work to work his garden.
He has a lantern. It is almost May,
the streetlights coming on, one to a corner.
If it is true the soul is other people,
then the antique finish of the thing
is how we love the past, how the aging
of a photograph becomes, like leaves, deciduous.
At the head of the stairs my mother's
mother's bedroom and beside hers the mahogany
and cedar of her father's . . . For a hundred years
the sun has set against the high side of the house.

I could climb those stairs, I could sleep and be
filled with the dead odors of moths and wools
and silks, with the sweet addictions of the flesh.
I could float a little lifetime above the kitchen talk,
branch, green, the sudden burden of the leaves.

Another November

In the blue eye of the medievalist there is a cart in the road.
There are brushfires and hedgerows and smoke and smoke
and the sun gold dollop going down.

The light has been falling all afternoon and the rain off and on.
There is a picture of a painting in a book in which the surface
of the paper, like the membrane of the canvas,

is nothing if not a light falling from another source.
The harvest is finished and figure, ground, trees lined up against
the sky all look like furniture—

even the man pushing the cart that looks like a chair,
even the people propped up in the fields, gleaning, or watching
the man, waving his passage on.

Part of a cloud has washed in to clarify or confound.
It is that time of the day between work and supper when the body
would lie down, like bread, or is so much of a piece

with the whole it is wood for a fire. Witness how
it is as difficult to paint rain as it is this light falling across
this page right now because there will always be

a plague of the luminous dead being wheeled to the edge of town.
The painting in the book is a landscape in a room, cart in the road,
someone's face at the window.

The Iron Lung

So this is the dust that passes through porcelain,
so this is the unwashed glass left over from supper,
so this is the air in the attic, in August,
and this the down on the breath of the sleeper. . . .

If we could fold our arms, but we can't.
If we could cross our legs, but we can't.
If we could put the mind to rest. . . .
But our fathers have set this task before us.

My face moons in the mirror, weightless,
without air, my head propped like a penny.
I'm dressed in a shoe, ready to walk out
of here. I'm wearing my father's body.

I remember my mother standing in the doorway
trying to tell me something. The day is thick
with the heat rising from the road. I am
too far away. She looks like my sister.

And I am dreaming of my mother in a doorway
telling my father to die or go away.
It is the front door, and my drunken father falls
to the porch on his knees like one of his children.

It is precisely at this moment I realize
I have polio and will never walk again.
And I am in the road on my knees, like my father,
but as if I were growing into the ground

I can neither move nor rise.
The neighborhood is gathering, and now
my father is lifting me into the ambulance
among the faces of my family. His face is

a blur or a bruise and he holds me
as if I had just been born. When I wake
I am breathing out of all proportion to myself.
My whole body is a lung; I am floating

above a doorway or a grave. And I know
I am in this breathing room as one
who understands how breath is passed
from father to son and passed back again.

At night, when my father comes to talk,
I tell him we have shared this body long enough.
He nods, like the speaker in a dream.
He knows that I know we're only talking.

Once there was a machine for breathing.
It would embrace the body and make a kind of love.
And when it was finished it would rise
like nothing at all above the earth

to drift through the daylight silence.
But at dark, in deep summer, if you thought you heard
something like your mother's voice calling you home,
you could lie down where you were and listen to the dead.

Rainbow

                                    Taking its time
through each of the seven vertebrae of light
the sun comes down. It is nineteen forty-nine.
You stand in the doorway drying your hands.
It is still summer, still raining.
The evening is everywhere gold: windows, grass,
the sun side of the trees. As if to speak
to someone you look back into the dark
of the house, call my name, go in. I know
I am dreaming again. Still, it is raining
and the sun shining . . . You come back out
into the doorway, shading your eyes. It looks
as if the whole sky is going down on one wing.
By now I have my hands above my eyes, listening.

Say Summer/For My Mother

I could give it back to you, perhaps in a season,
say summer. I could give you leaf back, green
grass, sky full of rain, root
that won't dig deeper, the names called out
just before sundown: *Linda back, Susy back,*
Carolyn. I could give you back supper
on the porch or the room without a breath
of fresh air, back the little tears in the heat,
the hot sleep on the kitchen floor,
back the talk in the great dark,
the voices low on the lawn
so the children can't hear,
say summer, say father, say mother:
Ruth and *Mary* and *Esther,* names in a book,
names I remember—I could give you back this name,
and back the breath to say it with—
we all know we'll die of our children—
back the tree bent over the water,
back the sun burning down,
back the witness back each morning.

Peppergrass

Nothing you could know, or name, or say
in your sleep, nothing you'd remember,
poor-man's-pepper, wildflower, weed—
what the guidebook calls *the side
of the road*—as from the moon the earth
looks beautifully anonymous, this field
pennycress, this shepherd's purse, nothing
you could see: summer nights we'd look up
at the absolute dark, the stars, and turn like toys. . . .

Nothing you could hold on to
but the wet grass, cold as morning.

We were windmills where the wind came from,
nothing, nothing you could name,
blowing the lights out, one by one.

For Esther

1

From the back it looks like a porch,
portable, the filigree railing French.

And Truman, Bess and the girl each come out
waving, in short sleeves, because the heat
is worse than Washington.

The day is twelve hours old, Truman is talking.
You tell me to pay attention,

               so I have my ball-
cap in my hands when he gets to the part that the sun

is suicidal, his dry voice barely audible above the train.

It makes a noise like steam.
He says, he says, he says.

His glasses silver in the sun. He says
there is never enough, and leans down to us.

2

Shultz and I put pennies on the track to make
the train jump. It jumps.

Afternoons you nap—one long pull of the body
through the heat.

                I go down to the depot
against orders; it's practically abandoned
except for the guy who hangs out

the mail and looks for pennies. He's president

of this place, he says. We pepper his B & O
brick building with tar balls when he's gone.

You hate the heat and sleep and let
your full voice go when I get caught.

You can't stand my noise or silence.
And I can hear a train in each bent coin.

You're thirty. I still seem to burden that young body.

3

Light bar, dark bar, all the way down. The trick is
if a train comes there is room for only the river.

I look down between the cross ties at the Great Miami.
Three miles back, near home,

Kessler has already climbed to his station.
The trick is waiting for the whistle.

                                                 I remember
your dream about bridges: how, as a child, they shook
you off, something the wind compelled.

You woke up holding on. And now this August morning

I don't know enough to be afraid or care.
I do my thinking here,

looking down at the long ladder on the water,
forty feet below.

4

The engine at idle, coasting in the yard, the call bell
back and forth, back and forth above the lull. . . .

I hang on like the mail as the cars lock in
to one another, couple, and make a train.

The time I break my arm you swear
me to the ground—no more rivers,
no more sidecar rides—

                  and stay up half
the night to rub my legs to sleep.

Sometimes you talk as if Roosevelt

were still alive. Recovery is memory.
I never broke my arm.

                  Back and forth. The names
of the states pass every day in front of us, single-file.

5

If a house were straw there'd be a wind,
if a house were wood there'd be a fire,

if a house were brick there'd be a track
and a train to tell the time.

                    I wish each passage
well—wind, fire, time, people on a train.
From here to there, three minutes, whistle-stop.

And the speech each night, the seconds clicking off.

The whole house shakes—or seems to. At intervals,
the ghost smoke fills

all the windows on the close-in side.
It's our weather. It's what we hear all night,
between Troy and anywhere, what you meant

to tell me, out of the body, out of the body travel.

Wrong Side of the River

I watched you on the wrong side
of the river, waving. You were trying
to tell me something. You used both hands
and sort of ran back and forth,
as if to say *look behind you, look out
behind you*. I wanted to wave back.
But you began shouting and I didn't
want you to think I understood.
So I did nothing but stand still,
thinking that's what to do on the wrong side
of the river. After a while you did too.
We stood like that for a long time. Then
I raised a hand, as if to be called on,
and you raised a hand, as if to the same question.

Out-of-the-Body Travel

And then he would lift this finest
of furniture to his big left shoulder
and tuck it in and draw the bow
so carefully as to make the music

almost visible on the air. And play
and play until a whole roomful of the sad
relatives mourned. They knew this was
drawing of blood, threading and rethreading

the needle. They saw even in my father's
face how well he understood the pain
he put them to—his raw red cheek
pressed against the cheek of the wood. . . .

2

And in one stroke he brings the hammer
down, like mercy, so that the young bull's
legs suddenly fly out from under it. . . .
While in the dream he is the good angel

in Chagall, the great ghost of his body
like light over the town. The violin
sustains him. It is pain remembered.
Either way, I know if I wake up cold,

and go out into the clear spring night,
still dark and precise with stars,
I will feel the wind coming down hard
like his hand, in fever, on my forehead.

Giraffe

The only head in the sky.
Buoyed like a bird's,
on bird legs too.
Moves in the slowmotion
of a ride
across the longlegged miles
of the same place.
Grazes in the trees.
Bends like a bow
over water
in a shy sort of
spreadeagle.
Embarrassed by
such vulnerability,
often trembles, gathering
together
in a single moment
the whole loose
fragment of body
before the run downwind.
Will stand still
in a camouflage of kind
in a rare daylight
for hours,
the leaves spilling
one break of sun
into another,
listening to the lions.
Will, when dark comes
and the fields open
until there are

no fields,
turn in the length
of light
toward some calm
still part of a tree's
new shadow, part of the moon.
Will stand all night
so tall
the sun will rise.

Now That My Father Lies Down Beside Me

We lie in that other darkness, ourselves.
There is less than the width of my left hand
between us. I can barely breathe,
but the light breathes easily,
wind on water across our two still bodies.

I cannot even turn to see him.
I would not touch him. Nor would I lift
my arm into the crescent of a moon.
(There is no star in the sky of this room,
only the light fashioning fish along the walls.
They swim and swallow one another.)

I dream we lie under water,
caught in our own sure drift.
A window, white shadow, trembles over us.
Light breaks into a moving circle.
He would not speak and I would not touch him.

It is an ocean under here.
Whatever two we were, we become
one falling body, one breath. Night lies down
at the sleeping center—no fish, no shadow,
no single, turning light. And I would not touch him
who lies deeper in the drifting dark than life.

Dedications

"Movie"/David Wyatt
"Catbird Beginning with a Cardinal"/Larry Levis
"Reading with the Poets"/Stanley Kunitz
"Will Work for Food"/Robert Penn Warren
"Cedar Waxwing on Scarlet Firethorn"/John Jones
"The Wyoming Poetry Circuit"/Gretel Ehrlich

About the Author

Stanley Plumly was born in Barnesville, Ohio, in 1939, and grew up in the lumber and farming regions of Virginia and Ohio. His work has been honored with the Delmore Schwartz Memorial Award and nominations for the National Book Critics Circle Award, the William Carlos Williams Award, and the Academy of American Poets' Lenore Marshall Poetry Prize. He has received a John Simon Guggenheim Foundation Fellowship, National Endowment for the Arts Awards, Pushcart Prizes, and an Ingram-Merrill Foundation Award. He has taught at many universities around the country, including the Universities of Iowa, Michigan, and Washington; Ohio University; Princeton; Columbia; the University of Houston; and New York University. He is currently a Distinguished University Professor and Professor of English at the University of Maryland.